simple STAINED GLASS *quilts*

simple STAINED GLASS *quilts*

Susan Purney Mark and Daphne Greig

CINCINNATI, OHIO

mycraftivity.com
CONNECT. CREATE. EXPLORE.

Other fine Krause Publications titles are available from your local bookstore, craft supply store, online retailer or visit our website at www.fwpublications.com.

12 11 10 09 08   5 4 3 2 1

DISTRIBUTED IN CANADA BY FRASER DIRECT
100 Armstrong Avenue
Georgetown, ON, Canada L7G 5S4
Tel: (905) 877-4411

DISTRIBUTED IN THE U.K. AND EUROPE BY DAVID & CHARLES
Brunel House, Newton Abbot, Devon, TQ12 4PU, England
Tel: (+44) 1626 323200, Fax: (+44) 1626 323319
Email: postmaster@davidandcharles.co.uk

DISTRIBUTED IN AUSTRALIA BY CAPRICORN LINK
P.O. Box 704, S. Windsor NSW, 2756 Australia
Tel: (02) 4577-3555

Library of Congress Cataloging in Publication Data
Greig, Daphne.
  Simple stained glass quilts / by Daphne Greig and Susan Purney Mark. --1st ed.
    p. cm.
  Includes index.
  ISBN-13: 978-0-89689-582-9 (pbk. : alk. paper)
  ISBN-10: 0-89689-582-3 (pbk. : alk. paper)
  1. Patchwork--Patterns. 2. Quilting--Patterns. I. Mark, Susan Purney. II. Title.
  TT835.G757 2008
  746.46'041--dc22
                    2008028722

Edited by Barbara Smith
Production Edited by Layne Vanover
Designed by Julie Barnett
Production coordinated by Matt Wagner

MEET THE AUTHORS

We began working together when we met over the cutting table of our local quilt shop, more than twelve years ago. We formed our company, Patchworks Studio, and began designing and publishing patterns together shortly afterward and have been creating our Too Easy Stained Glass patterns since 2003. We teach the technique all across North America to excited quiltmakers who loudly exclaim, "It's too easy!" This book was, for us, a natural evolution. It gives us the opportunity to explore design and fabric options in detail. We love bringing a variety of designs and techniques into print in books, patterns and magazines and have a great many ideas stored up for future publication.

We live in Victoria, British Columbia, where we love to garden, walk and explore our beautiful native land. We also spend part of each year traveling and teaching. Please send us pictures of your Too Easy Stained Glass projects. We'd love to hear from you! You can contact Susan and Daphne at:

Patchworks Studio
2552 Eastdowne Road
Victoria, BC V8R 5P9
Canada
Phone: 250-595-4411
Web: www.patchworkstudio.com

ACKNOWLEDGMENTS

No creative endeavor is made in isolation, and this book is no exception. Eight years ago, we developed our first Too Easy Stained Glass patterns, and we were truly overwhelmed by the response from our retail customers and quilt shops. They have supported us in so many ways by providing suggestions for design ideas and magazine articles, and ongoing encouragement for our concept.

We want to thank all the quilt shops that ordered our patterns and the teachers who taught them. We also appreciate the innumerable kind comments about the designs and the technique. This book was written primarily because of all the requests for a book. Our retail customers, who could see the versatility and the many possibilities for our six Too Easy steps, have been the impetus for writing this book. Thanks also go to Lynne Allaire for thinking of stained glass when she traveled to Paris. Our Paris View quilts, *Serenity Bridge* (page 72) and *Rose Arbor* (page 74), along with the *West Coast Landscape* variation (page 80), are the result of her kindness.

Our special thanks go to book acquisitions editor Candy Wiza, who, very early on, saw the concept as a book, and to Toni Toomey, who gently walked us through the steps to bring the concept to print. Special thanks are also due to Barbara Smith, our editor. We are thrilled to once again work with such a professional and conscientious person. We also want to thank our photographers: J.D. Wacker for our step-by-step pictures and for welcoming us to a Wisconsin winter, and Coral Gilbert for our lovely portraits. And thanks go to Krause Publications and their staff for being a great team.

Each and every quilter is a creative person, but we couldn't work without all the wonderful products from our suppliers—many thanks to each and every one. Their Web sites are listed in the Resources section at the back of the book.

Our husbands, Henry and Alan, once again filled the breach with cooking, laundry and often, the needed words to keep us on track—much love and many thanks to you both.

METRIC CONVERSION CHART

To convert	to	multiply by
inches	centimeters	2.54
centimeters	inches	0.4
feet	centimeters	30.5
centimeters	feet	0.03
yards	meters	0.9
meters	yards	1.1

TABLE *of* CONTENTS

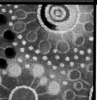

This book offers an easy-to-master, versatile technique, which lends itself to many different designs and styles. The patterns can be interchanged to provide multiple options for size and layout combinations. The projects range from small to large and provide great uses for a wide variety of fabrics: scenic prints, batiks, floral fabrics and even photographs printed on fabric. The six Too Easy steps show you how to achieve great success with stunning results in a short period of time.

If this is your first introduction to our stained glass method, we recommend that you begin with a small project. *From My Window* is a small quilt, perfect for learning our technique. The project begins on page 30. After you have mastered the technique, flip through the projects and your fabrics. You'll find a vast array of designs to get your creative juices flowing.

inspiration

Stained glass windows have always held a particular fascination for us, and we've been fortunate to develop a terrific technique that makes their construction just Too Easy! As you work through this book, you'll see we've been inspired by a whole range of designs from very unlikely places. We encourage you to look around to find some possibilities for creating exciting quilts.

Of course, you can always use actual stained glass windows as inspiration, but perhaps you don't have any near you. There are many great books full of designs to inspire you to create your own unique projects using our Too Easy method. Magazine and newspaper articles about architecture and advertisements for a range of products can inspire you. We also found interesting and useful designs in continuous-line quilting patterns and quilt-design software.

Sometimes we like to work with a theme, such as a forest or mountains. We have also found designs in things around our homes. Have a look at your china cabinet, fireplace or heating grates. By repeating the various design elements found in these items, you can make many interesting motifs.

Jewelry can offer a lot of ideas, so be sure to look through your earrings, bracelets, and necklaces.

If you're traveling, look for interesting ironwork and details around doors and windows. Many designs will have features that can be adapted to make wonderful stained glass quilts.

Chapter One

TOO EASY TOOLS AND MATERIALS

The tools you'll need for the projects are easy to locate. You probably already have most of them in your collection. Visit your local quilt shop or shop online for any of the items you are missing.

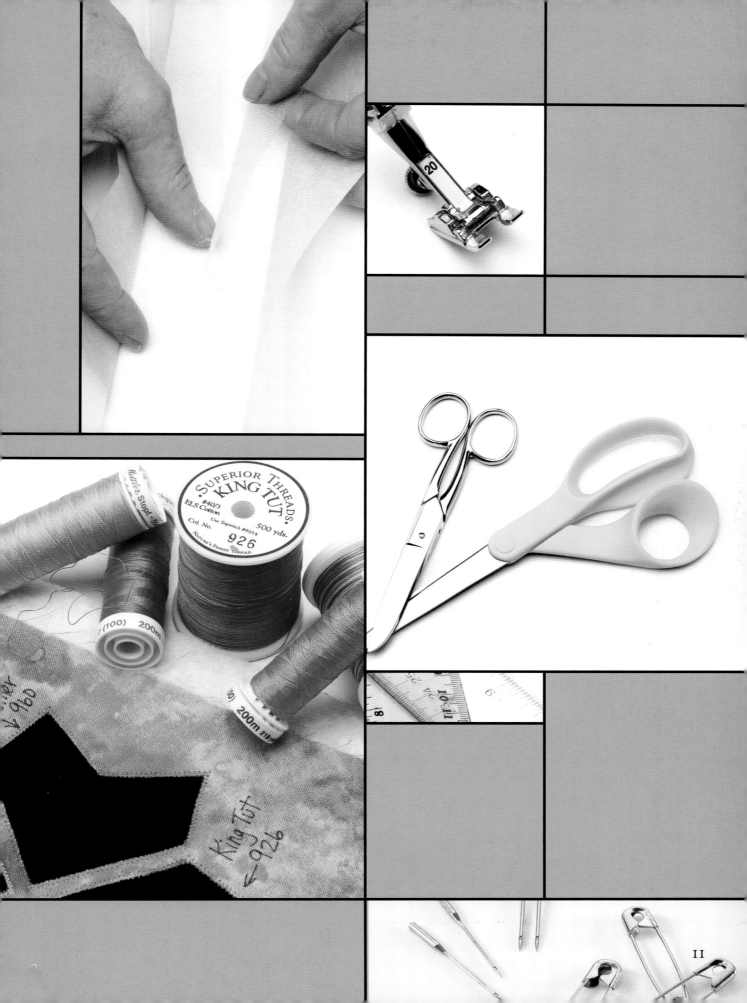

FUSIBLE WEB

Fusible web is the key ingredient for making your Too Easy Stained Glass projects, and it's the ingredient that sets this technique apart from the other labor-intensive methods requiring freezer paper, glued edges or expensive bias tape. Fusible web comes in a range of types, almost all of them attached to a release paper that stays attached until after the ironing process.

In our experience, Steam-A-Seam 2 is the best fusible web for these projects. It's a relatively heavy web with release paper on both sides. The paper keeps the web from sticking to the pattern when you trace it, and it won't separate from the fusible web until you want it to. If you try another brand, choose a fusible web that can be sewn. If you're planning to make a project that will be washed, make certain the fusible web can be washed as well. If you're unsure about whether you can sew and wash a web, we recommend testing it before using it in your projects.

Fusible web comes in a range of sizes. Generally, you can buy 12", 18" or 24" widths, which are cut from rolls. If you decide to make many stained glass projects, it might be a good idea to buy a whole roll.

For large stained glass projects, you may have to join pieces of fusible web together before tracing the pattern. To join pieces of Steam-A-Seam 2, you can fold the release paper back to expose the fusible web on both pieces to be joined. Then layer approximately 1" of one piece on top of the other, replace the release paper and finger-press the area.

You can also staple or pin web pieces together. Masking tape will hold the pieces together, but cellophane tape will not stick to the release paper.

Another method for creating projects that are larger than your fusible web is to make four copies of the design and fuse them separately to one large

Fusible Web Products

We find excellent advice about fusible web products at our local quilt shops, and we test the products before using them in our projects.

piece of the stained glass leading fabric (usually black). This method is used for the *Spinning Wheel* quilts on pages 62 and 66.

We recommend that you keep your fusible web rolled rather than folded so it won't separate from the release paper. Large web pieces can be rolled onto a pipe or tube. Your local quilt shop may have an empty fabric bolt cardboard they would be happy to give you.

Many fusible webs are sold with a plastic instruction sheet wrapped around them. Keep this sheet with your fusible web to remind you of the brand and type, because fusing instructions may vary for different products.

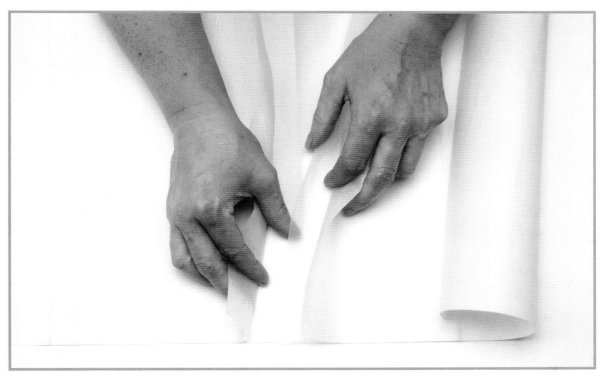

Joining Fusible Web

To join pieces of fusible web to use with larger designs, layer the web and finger-press the fusible layers together.

Here is an example of web pieces pinned together.

We roll long lengths of fusible web around fabric bolt cardboard found at our local quilt shop.

TRACING TOOLS

You will trace the pattern design onto the release paper of the fusible web. Listed below are the tools you will need for this step.

PENCILS OR MARKERS

You will need a sharp pencil for tracing your pattern. We like mechanical pencils (cheaper by the dozen) for tracing the design. If you use a regular pencil, be sure to have a good pencil sharpener; the pencil lead will quickly dull, and it's important to use a sharp pencil to trace the design lines accurately. Use a hard-lead pencil, HB or higher, and don't forget an eraser in case you make a mistake. We use white gum artist's erasers, but any school-type eraser will work.

You could also use a fine-point permanent marker, like the Sharpie brand. Test your marker to be sure it dries quickly without smudging.

RULER

For tracing straight lines, you'll need a clear plastic or drafting ruler with a minimum length of 18". Look for this ruler at an art or office supply store. These rulers are easier to use than rotary cutting rulers because they are thinner and you can see the edge to trace accurately.

Use a drafting ruler for tracing.

Regular pencils, mechanical pencils or fine-point permanent markers can be used to trace the pattern.

IRONING TOOLS

The traced design will be ironed or fused to the fabric used for leading. Here are the tools you will need for the fusing step.

PRESSING SURFACE

You can use a regular ironing board when you iron the traced fusible web to the leading fabric. Sometimes, it's easier to have a larger surface for ironing the web to the fabric. You can create a temporary pressing surface by covering your sewing table with several layers of batting and an old sheet or piece of muslin. Always layer enough batting to protect your table from the heat.

IRON

An iron is another important tool for your projects. We do not use the mini craft irons—they don't get hot enough for good fusing. We have used a smaller travel iron with success, and you may want to try this if you have one. You don't

need to use steam for our stained glass method because the pressing sheet and release papers will act as a vapor barrier.

You might consider having a dedicated iron for your fusible projects. Have a look at your local thrift shop for this inexpensive addition to your sewing room.

PRESSING SHEET

A pressing sheet is an absolute must for your stained glass quilts. It will save your iron, your ironing surface and your good silk blouse! Sometimes what transfers to the bottom of your iron is not the fusible web, but the pencil marks. That can be frustrating the next time you use your iron because black marks may appear on the fabric.

Teflon pressing sheets are made to withstand high temperatures and, while they are not inexpensive, they are an important investment. Well cared for, they will last a long time. They can be cleaned by hand washing or by wiping them with a clean cloth. Buy the largest size sheet you can find.

We use a Teflon pressing sheet to protect our irons from fusible web and pencil marks.

CUTTING TOOLS

After you have fused the traced design to your leading fabric, you will cut the fused fabric, leaving just the ¼" leading lines. You'll spend some time cutting out the open areas in your leading, and there are a variety of cutting tools for you to choose from. Here are our recommendations.

SCISSORS

Using the right tool for the job can make all the difference in how much you enjoy the process. Scissors are no exception. Look for scissors that are sharp right out to the point, not those with blunt tips. We use medium-sized scissors, not large shears, and choose ones that feel comfortable in the hand. We also use smaller sharp-to-the-point scissors for cutting small areas.

Clean and sharpen your scissors regularly. Remove any sticky residue that builds up from the fusible web. We use a small amount of nail polish remover on a cotton pad to clean the blades of our scissors.

ROTARY CUTTER

We often use a very small rotary cutter when cutting our fused fabric. The 18mm size is easy to control and maneuver, and we can cut close to the corners. We just snip the last part of the corner with our small, sharp scissors. We like to cut the curved areas freehand, and we have more control with the little rotary cutter.

We use the 45mm cutter for long, straight areas in a design. You will also need a rotary-cutting

Sharp, medium-sized scissors are useful for cutting fused fabric. Smaller scissors can clip into the corners and smaller areas to make perfect cuts.

A small rotary cutter or art knife can be used with a rotary ruler and can also be used to cut curves freehand.

ruler to cut against for the straight lines. Remember to change the blade regularly, but also clean the blade often by removing it from the cutter and wiping it clean with a small piece of batting.

ART KNIFE

Another cutting tool that works well for stained glass projects is an art knife. These are commonly found in office or art supply stores. Replacement blades are available so you can change the blade when it becomes dull. Be extra careful with the knife and remember to cover the blade when not in use, just as you do with your rotary cutter.

The advantage with the knife is you can cut right into a corner, which is difficult with a rotary cutter. Daphne likes to use the Add-a-Quarter ruler when cutting straight lines with her art knife because it is easier to hold securely, and the lip on the ruler helps her cut the leading at exactly ¼".

Both the rotary cutter and the art knife must be used with a self-healing cutting mat. These are available in many brands and sizes. We have large mats (24" × 36") that we use for cutting at home and smaller ones (18" × 24") for taking to workshops. Store your mat flat and it will last for years.

We like to use a low-loft, cotton/polyester blend batting for all our quilts. The brand we use is lightly needle-punched to lock the fibers together, and it has a light resin finish to resist bearding. Bearding is just as the name implies: little "beards" of batting poking through your quilt fabric. We want to use a batting that does not beard, especially with the black fabrics we often use for our stained glass quilts. Our batting is washable, but we don't pre-wash it because our quilted wall hangings won't be washed.

Black batting is also available. If you choose this type, be sure the color doesn't show through any light focus fabrics.

Our stitch of choice for sewing leading is a zig-zag. Most sewing machines have a zigzag stitch that is adjustable in both width and length. You don't need any other special stitches for the projects.

It's helpful to have an open-toe foot for your sewing machine so you can clearly see where you are stitching. If one is not included in the sewing machine feet that came with your machine, contact your local dealer to see if one is available.

We like to use an open-toe foot to see where we need to stitch.

THREAD

Choose a variety of decorative threads for quilting your projects.

The stitching line holding the leading fabric in place on top of the focus fabric is a narrow zigzag stitch. The focus of your project should be on the overall design, not the thread. We recommend a machine-embroidery cotton thread, commonly called a 60 weight. This weight creates a nice stitch without bulk.

We use black cotton fabric for the leading in most of our projects. However, sometimes using a different color for the leading is a better design option. We try to match the thread color as close as possible to the leading fabric color. This is fairly simple when the fabric is a solid or tone-on-tone print. If you use a fabric with several colors, selecting a thread can be more challenging. For *Princess Rose*, page 116, Daphne selected a mottled, multicolored fabric for the leading. She wanted to be sure the zigzag stitching blended with the fabric, so she created a small sample to test a variety of threads. She wrote the names and numbers of the threads right on the sample as she tested them and then made her choice.

You may also need threads for quilting where there are large unstitched areas in the design. Choose fine threads like rayon, polyester or invisible thread. Other options include heavier variegated threads, which add shading and dimension to your projects.

Test several threads on a small sample when using multicolored leading fabric.

Since the leading stitching lines and the main quilting lines are the same, you can save time by stitching them both at the same time. Stitching through all three layers of the quilt sandwich and the fusible web requires a sturdy needle. We choose either quilting needles or embroidery needles. We use size 75/11 with 60-weight thread and larger sizes, 80/12 or 90/14, with heavier decorative threads. We begin each new project with a fresh needle and make sure the needle is properly inserted into the machine before we begin stitching.

Some people like to use a twin needle for our stained glass method. This will work only if you use a straight stitch, rather than a zigzag. Always check the space between your twin needles because some will be too wide for the leading. We recommend making a test sample first before you decide to use a twin needle.

No matter which fusible web you buy, you'll probably have some sticky residue buildup on your needle. Remove it by wiping the needle with a little piece (about 1" square) of batting. Be careful to take your foot off the pedal when you do this, to prevent stitching through your finger!

We like to pin-baste our quilts in preparation for quilting. We use straight medium-sized rustproof safety pins (size no. 2). Smaller, curved pins are also available. Use the ones you like best.

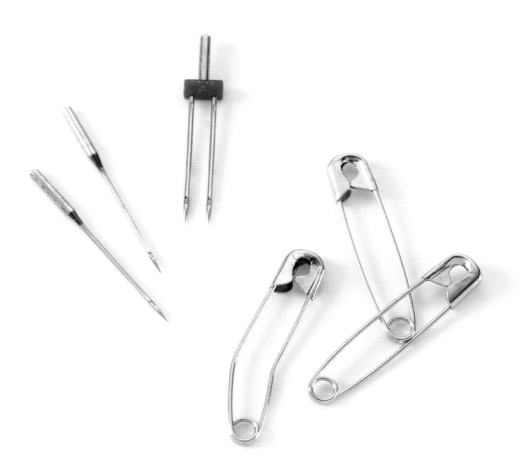

QUILTING MARKERS

We use both water-soluble blue markers and white ink markers for marking quilting designs, and in some cases, for marking positioning lines on the leading fabric. You'll need the blue markers most often to mark on the focus fabrics, and the white markers on the black fabric. Read and follow the manufacturer's instructions for removal. Always test your markers on the fabric you are using to be sure they can be removed.

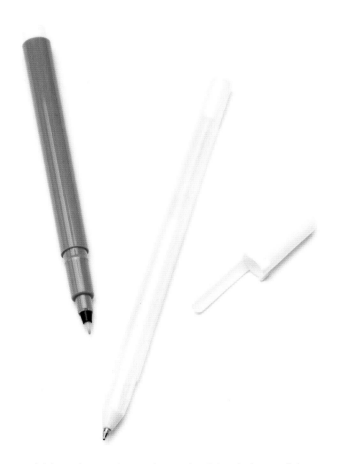

Water-soluble markers can be used to mark quilting designs on light-colored focus fabrics, while white ink markers work best for dark fabrics.

Chapter Two

FABRIC CHOICES

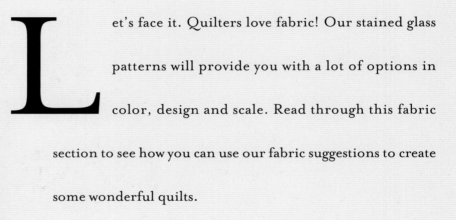

Let's face it. Quilters love fabric! Our stained glass patterns will provide you with a lot of options in color, design and scale. Read through this fabric section to see how you can use our fabric suggestions to create some wonderful quilts.

Quilt shops are always a delight for the eyes, and they are wonderful places to discover the latest and most exciting fabrics and products. Take some time to explore your local shop. Imagine the projects you can create after you have looked at the quilt projects, beginning on page 30.

Landscape fabrics can convey certain feelings and are available in just about every conceivable subject—from the high Arctic with polar bears and icebergs to exotic jungles with colorful creatures peering out from palm leaves. We've also found a lovely grouping of European café scenes … ooh la la!

There are many fabric companies designing scenic prints, and although you love them, you may ask, what can I do with them? We have the perfect solution with our stained glass quilts.

Look for a variety of different sizes and scales of landscape fabrics. Don't worry too much about the fabric being the correct scale or size. We've given you several ideas in the project chapters to make small changes so the stained glass design will fit the fabric you choose.

Look for variety in scale and design.

Consider using a printed panel for your project.

For another focus fabric option, consider the wide range of scenic printed panels available. We used lovely cushion panels for *Venetian Glass* (page 44).

OTHER FOCUS FABRICS

Perhaps a landscape fabric isn't for you. Other choices include seasonal, floral and other prints. Maybe you would like to create your own focus fabric by piecing together a variety of fabrics or by printing a photograph on fabric.

   Deciding which fabric to use can take time. Perhaps you may find the perfect one right away and know exactly which of our stained glass patterns to use. Sometimes you may find a great fabric and buy it without having a solid plan. Now is the time to check your stash and see what fabric might be a perfect fit for one of the stained glass designs.

Use your family photos in a stained glass design.

Piecing your focus fabric is a great option.

Other focus fabrics.

Placing a stained glass design over a fabric gives you a different view of the fabric. The stained glass leading lines will draw you into the focus fabric so you really see what is included in the fabric print. We encourage you to try placing your cut leading design over several focus fabric choices. This is what we mean by auditioning your fabrics.

For landscape fabrics, there may be a focal point in the fabric design. You can move the stained glass leading around on the focus fabric to select the best image. Think of the leading as a frame around a picture. The frame draws your eye to what is happening in the picture. Most often, you have several choices of where to place the leading over a landscape. It's usually best to place the focus fabric feature off center.

Another option is to change the leading design by lengthening or shortening it to suit a particular fabric. See the Paris View quilts on pages 72, 74 and 80 for several versions of a leading design.

You can also use just part of the leading design. In the Rose Window projects on page 108, three designs were created from the original leading design.

See how different the fabrics can look with the leading design on top.

Good

Better

Best

Move the leading around to find the best position: good, better, best.

POOR FABRIC CHOICES

Some focus fabrics do not work well for stained glass designs. For example, directional fabrics and stripes are not suitable for circular designs. Checks and plaids provide texture, but placing them in stained glass designs doesn't enhance their character in any way. However, these fabrics can be used for accent borders.

These fabrics don't work well.

LEADING FABRICS

While we traditionally think of using black fabric for the stained glass leading, it isn't the only choice. In some of our designs, we have used other fabrics. We're sure you'll agree they are equally effective. Consider choosing a different solid color, a very small-scale print or a textural or tone-on-tone fabric. The colors in the print should be close in value. We have also used fabric that is shaded from selvage to selvage and fabric that we have darkened in a tea bath. Have fun being creative, and try a range of fabrics. Whatever your choice might be for the leading, choose a fabric with a high thread count and one that doesn't fray easily.

Think of other fabrics to use for the leading.

SOLID BLACK

If you choose solid black for the leading in your stained glass quilt, there are some factors to keep in mind. Many different black fabrics are available, and some are more intense than others. Examine several at your local quilt shop and see how different the black fabrics look, especially when compared to one another. We prefer Black Jet by Michael Miller Fabrics because of the intensity of the color.

Remember to use the same black fabric for all parts of the quilt: the leading design, borders and binding. If you're making two quilts to match (for example, a wall hanging and a table runner), use the same black fabric for both pieces. There can be a striking difference between a border and a binding if two different black fabrics are used.

We recommend keeping track of the black fabric you use. Cut a snip of the fabric and label it with the manufacturer's name, the style number and where you bought it.

Black fabrics can be very different.

Black fabric can fade over time when exposed to strong light, especially sunlight. We recommend that your wall hangings not be placed in areas where they get direct sun. Ultraviolet filters on your windows can decrease the sun damage. Test your fabrics by taping a small piece to your sunniest window and compare it with the original fabric after a couple of days.

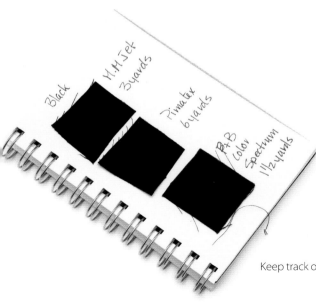

Keep track of black fabrics in a notebook.

Chapter Three

TOO EASY STEP BY STEP: YOUR FIRST PROJECT

This section explains the Too Easy steps you will need to follow when making the projects. We recommend that you first make this quilt, *From My Window*, to become familiar with the technique before you begin any of the other projects. We used a scenic print for our quilt, but you can try other types of fabric in your window. Review the Fabric Choices section on page 22 for ideas.

FROM MY WINDOW · *Designed and made by Susan and Daphne* · *Finished size: 13" × 15½"*

FROM MY WINDOW

materials

LEADING FABRIC:
1⅛ yd. black cotton, includes outer border, backing, and binding

FOCUS FABRIC:
fat quarter, 18" × 22"

ACCENT FABRIC FOR INNER BORDER:
⅛ yd.

FUSIBLE WEB:
8½" × 11"

LOW−LOFT BATTING:
16" × 18½"

MACHINE EMBROIDERY THREAD:
black 60 weight

Making the Quilt Top

1 Tape the *From My Window* pattern, from the pattern sheet, to a table. Center the fusible web, paper side up, over the pattern.

With Steam-A-Seam 2, check to see which paper liner is removed first by peeling apart a tiny section at the corner. Trace on the liner that stays attached to the web.

2 Center the design on the web and with a pencil or fine permanent marker, trace the pattern onto the web. Smoothly trace the curves and use a ruler to trace the straight lines.

3 From the leading fabric, cut a rectangle 11" × 13½", and press.

4 Center the traced pattern on the wrong side of the leading rectangle. Cover the fusible web with your pressing sheet and fuse together, following the web manufacturer's instructions. Be sure all the edges are fused well.

5 Let the fused fabrics cool. Use your rotary cutter, scissors or art knife to cut the open areas in the leading fabric.

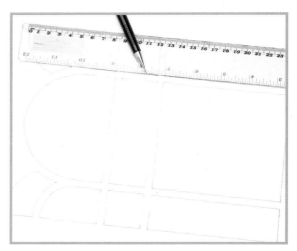

Trace the leading design onto the fusible web.

Fuse the design to the black leading fabric.

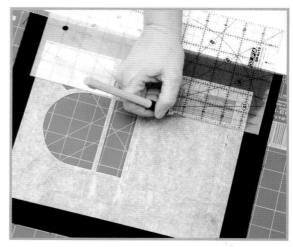

Cut the open areas to create the leading.

Fuse the leading in place.

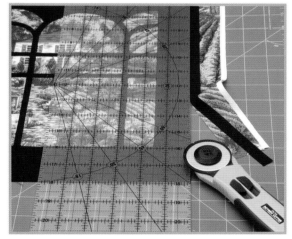

Trim around the focus fabric.

Add the accent and outer borders.

Be sure to cut smooth curves and maintain the ¼" leading lines. Use a ruler when cutting the straight lines of the design.

6 Lay the fabric, right side up, on your pressing surface and press it well. (See Pressing Surface, page 15.)

7 Remove the paper backing from the leading and position the leading over the focus fabric. Move the leading around to different areas of the focus fabric until you are happy with the effect.

Make certain there are no puckers or folds in either fabric and the leading lines are straight.

8 Cover the leading with your pressing sheet and fuse, following the manufacturer's instructions. Be sure all the edges are fused well. Let the fabrics cool.

9 With the piece right side up, measure 1½" from the outside edges of the focus fabric and trim away the excess leading and focus fabric.

10 On the wrong side, use sharp scissors to trim away any excess focus fabric that is not fused around the outer edges.

Adding Borders

1 Cut all strips selvage to selvage. Use ¼" seam allowances to sew the border strips to the quilt. From the accent fabric, cut three ¾" strips for the inner border. Measure the quilt length and cut two border pieces to that measurement. Sew them to the sides of the quilt. Press the allowances toward the accent strips.

2 Measure the quilt width and cut two border pieces to that measurement. Sew them to the top and bottom of the quilt. Press the allowances toward the accent strips.

3 For the outer border, cut two strips of leading fabric 2" wide. Add them to the quilt in the same manner as the accent strips. Press the allowances toward the accent strips.

Quilting

1 From the leading fabric, cut a piece 16" × 18½" for the backing.

2 Sandwich the backing (wrong side up), batting (either side up) and quilt top (right side up) and baste the layers well with safety pins.

3 Thread your sewing machine, in the top and bobbin, with black embroidery thread. Set your machine to a narrow zigzag stitch.

4 Make a couple of layered samples with light colored fabric to test the stitch width and length.

We recommend using an open-toe foot for the samples and stitching the leading of your project. Make a note of your machine settings for future projects.

5 Begin in the center of the quilt and stitch on both edges of each leading line. Remove pins as necessary while you sew.

Place the leading to the left of the needle and stitch so most of the zigzag lies on the black fabric. Begin and end each line of stitching with a couple of backstitches and remove pins as necessary.

6 Use a straight stitch in the ditch on both sides of the accent border. You may choose to add decorative stitching or additional quilting in the borders for emphasis.

7 Press the quilt lightly when all the stitching is complete.

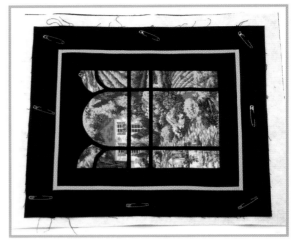

Pin-baste the quilt layers together.

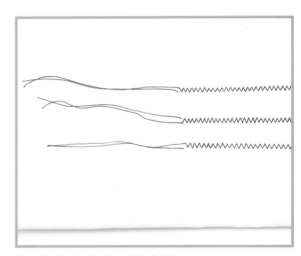

Test the zigzag stitch on light fabric.

Pivot the stitching at the corners. Our photograph shows the white stitching so it is easier to see. Use thread matching the leading for your quilt.

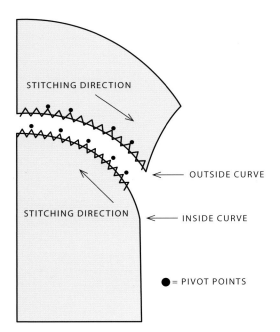

STITCHING DIRECTION

OUTSIDE CURVE

STITCHING DIRECTION

INSIDE CURVE

● = PIVOT POINTS

Pivot on the right side for outside curves, on the left side for inside curves.

Stitching Curves

For smooth curves, you will have to stop and pivot the work as you sew. The tighter the curve, the more frequently you'll need to pivot. It's important that the needle remains in the fabric when you lift the presser foot to turn the work. Use the needle-down option if your machine has one. It is also important that the needle is in the correct position when you turn your work. These are the pivot points.

For outside curves, pivot when the needle is on the outside of the curve; that is, on the right-hand swing of the zigzag stitch.

Binding

1 Cut two strips of leading fabric 2¼", from selvage to selvage, for the binding. Join the strips on the short ends with 45-degree seams. Press the seam allowances open to reduce bulk.

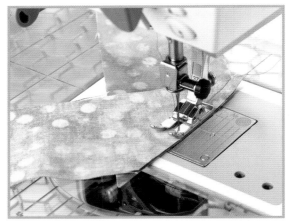

Join the binding strips with 45-degree seams. (Green binding was used in the photo so you can see it better. You will probably want to use black for your project.)

Finish one beginning end of the binding strip.

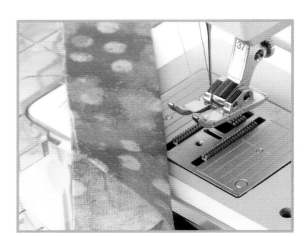

Fold the strip in half, right side out, and press.

2 Cut the beginning end of the binding strip at a 45-degree angle and fold under ¼" of the beginning end to make a finished edge.

3 Fold the binding in half along its length, wrong sides together, matching the long raw edges; press.

4 With the quilt right side up, and starting in the middle of one side of the quilt, align the raw edges of the binding strip with the raw edges of one side of the quilt.

5 Leaving about 3" of the beginning end free, stitch the binding to the quilt, through all layers, about ¼" in from the raw edges. Stop sewing ¼" from the corner and backstitch three or four stitches.

6 Slide the quilt from under the presser foot and fold the binding up at a 45-degree angle. Then fold the binding down, as shown, and align it with the second side of the quilt.

7 Starting at the fold, continue sewing the binding to the quilt. Repeat the folding steps at each corner.

8 When you stitch the last side, stop about 3" from where you began sewing the binding.

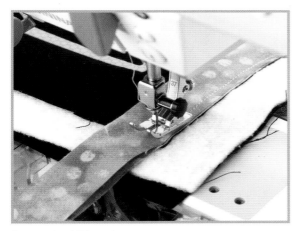

Stop sewing ¼" from the corner.

Fold the binding to make a mitered corner, then continue sewing.

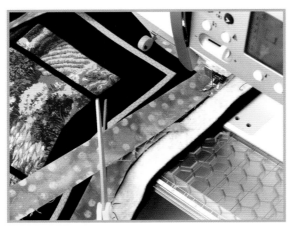

Using the angle of the beginning end as a guide, trim the tail end, leaving about 1½" of overlap.

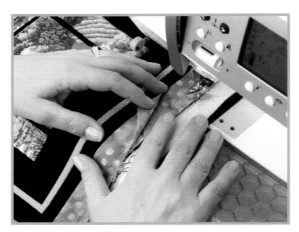

Tuck the tail end inside the beginning end.

9 Use your scissors to cut the tail end at a 45-degree angle, leaving 1½" to overlap the beginning end.

10 Tuck the tail end inside the beginning end. Smooth the ends in place, then finish sewing them to the quilt. Backstitch to lock the threads.

11 Trim the excess batting and backing even with the quilt edges, being careful not to cut into the binding. Turn the binding to the back of the quilt and slipstitch it in place by hand.

To make the miter at each corner, make a 45-degree fold in the binding and secure the intersection with a stitch.

Slipstitch the binding in place on the wrong side.

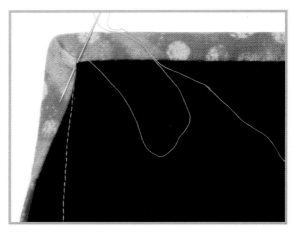

Make a miter at each corner.

Making a Hanging Sleeve

1 To hang your window quilt, you can sew a sleeve onto the back. A small wooden rod or curtain rod can then be slipped into the sleeve and the rod placed on hooks or small nails. We make our sleeves with a tube of fabric, finished at both ends and about 1" narrower (after finishing the ends) than the top edge of the quilt.

Cut a piece of backing fabric that measures 4" wide by the width of the quilt.

For larger quilts, use a wider strip (6" to 8") of backing fabric to allow space for a larger rod to support the weight of the quilt.

2 Finish the two short edges by folding ¼" to the wrong side twice and topstitching the folds.

3 Fold the strip in half, wrong sides together, and join the raw edges with a ½" seam allowance. Press the allowances open. Flatten the tube, centering the seam on what will be the back of the tube.

4 Pin the sleeve to the quilt back, with the seam hidden at the back, and align the top edge of the sleeve with the top of the quilt, just below the binding. Center the sleeve across the width. Slipstitch the top edge of the sleeve in place securely.

5 Push the bottom edge of the tube up about ½" so the tube doesn't lie flat, which will allow room for the inserted rod. Pin the bottom edge in place and slipstitch the edge securely.

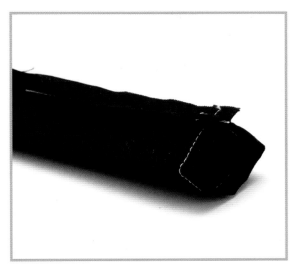

Finish the end of the sleeve, then sew to make a tube. Press with the seam centered on the back.

Adding a Label

1 Adding a label to the back of your quilt is the finishing touch. It can be as simple as a rectangle of muslin with your name and date written with a permanent marker, or it can be a work of art. We like to print our quilt labels by using printable fabric in our inkjet printer. For small quilts, like *From My Window*, you can fuse the label to the back. If you prefer, you can finish the edges of your label and stitch it in place by hand.

Additional Options

Be creative! Too Easy Stained Glass designs lend themselves to making your own statement with additional options. Personalize your project by adding mementos from your travels or cherished events. Here are some creative ideas to get you started.

Quilt designs in the borders with decorative threads.

Cut some elements from the focus fabric and appliqué them onto the border. Use fusible web and a narrow zigzag stitch to fasten them down.

Embellish the quilt with beads, buttons or crystals. Use the theme of the fabric for ideas.

Add more borders in contrasting colors. Use different border widths for visual interest and to keep the design in proportion.

Quilt around parts of the scene for added dimension.

Chapter Four

LANDSCAPE PROJECTS

Gaze through your window onto a luscious landscape! By using our method you can create wonderful scenes of real or imagined vistas. Have fun visiting some European vineyards, safari adventures, wilderness treks or Asian skylines with your landscape projects.

VENETIAN GLASS · *Designed and made by Susan* · *Finished size : 22" × 22"*

VENETIAN GLASS

Memories of the Italian countryside inspired this simple yet classic design seen on page 43. In your project, you can showcase a fabric that inspires you or, as done in this quilt, use a great printed panel.

This leading design was inspired by a simple edging pattern Susan found in the stained glass window of a friend's Arts and Crafts-style bungalow. Remember to look all around you for ideas to create your own unique leading patterns. You could find exciting patterns in carved woodwork, home decorating fabrics or even carpeting.

materials

LEADING FABRIC:
1¾ yd. black cotton, includes outer border, backing and binding

FOCUS FABRIC OR PRINTED PANEL:
½ yd.

ACCENT FABRIC FOR INNER BORDER:
⅛ yd.

FUSIBLE WEB:
16" × 16"

LOW-LOFT BATTING:
25" × 25"

MACHINE EMBROIDERY THREAD:
black 60 weight

Making the Quilt Top

1 Tape the *Venetian Glass* pattern from the pattern sheet to your table. Center the fusible web, paper side up, over the pattern and trace the design.

Use a ruler to trace the straight lines.

2 Cut an 18" square of leading fabric. Press it well to remove puckers and wrinkles.

3 Center the traced design on the wrong side of the leading square. Cover the fusible web with your pressing sheet and fuse, following the web manufacturer's instructions. Be sure all edges are fused well.

4 Let the piece cool then use your rotary cutter, scissors or art knife to cut the open areas of the design.

Use a ruler when cutting the straight lines of the design and to maintain the ¼" leading lines.

5 Cut an 18" square of focus fabric. Place it on your ironing surface and press to remove any puckers or wrinkles.

6 Carefully remove the paper backing and position the leading over the focus fabric. Move the leading around until you are pleased with the placement.

Make sure all fusible areas of the leading are positioned over the focus fabric. Also check that all straight design lines are straight.

7 Cover the piece with your pressing sheet and fuse the leading to the focus fabric. Be careful that you don't move the leading during this step. Let the fused fabrics cool.

8 With the piece right side up, measure 1½" from the outside edges of the focus fabric and trim the excess leading fabric.

9 On the wrong side, use sharp scissors to trim away any excess focus fabric that is not fused around the outer edges.

Adding Borders

1 Cut all strips selvage to selvage. From the accent fabric, cut two strips 1½" wide for the inner border. Measure the quilt length and cut two pieces to that measurement. Sew them to the sides of the quilt. Press the allowances toward the accent strips.

2 Measure the quilt width and cut two pieces to that measurement. Sew them to the top and bottom. Press the allowances toward the accent strips.

3 For the outer border, cut four 2½" strips of leading fabric. Add them to the quilt in the same manner as the accent strips. Press the seam allowances toward the accent strips.

Quilting and Finishing

1 Cut a piece of leading fabric 25"× 25" for the backing.

2 Sandwich the quilt top, batting and backing together and baste well with safety pins.

3 Thread your sewing machine, in the top and bobbin, with the embroidery thread. Set your machine to a narrow zigzag stitch.

4 Begin in the center of the quilt and stitch on both edges of each leading line. Remove pins as necessary while you sew.

5 Remove all remaining pins and square up the wall hanging to measure 22" × 22".

6 Cut three strips of leading fabric 2¼" wide for binding. Join the strips on the short ends with 45-degree seams. Press the seam allowances open to reduce bulk.

7 Fold the binding in half lengthwise, wrong sides together, and apply the binding all around the raw edges, mitering the corners.

8 Turn the binding to the back and slipstitch it in place by hand.

9 Add a sleeve and label to the back of your wall hanging.

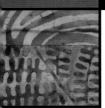

Living on the west coast of Canada, Susan is influenced by the scenery of forests, streams, mountains and wildlife, as you can see in this quilt. This wall hanging design can showcase many of the fabrics you'll find in local shops. You can choose to create your own focus fabric by joining strips to make a landscape, or use a printed panel. Look for buttons or interesting threads to add details to your quilt.

Choose six focus fabrics with values from very light to dark. Fabrics that would work well include batiks, subtle prints, Fossil Fern fabrics, or ones with a suggestion of leaves, sky, sunsets or trees.

materials

LEADING FABRIC:
1¾ yd. black cotton, includes outer border, backing and binding

FOCUS FABRIC:
6 types, totaling ⅝ yd., includes inner border

FUSIBLE WEB:
16" × 18"

LOW-LOFT BATTING:
23" × 26"

MACHINE EMBROIDERY THREAD:
black 60 weight

Making the Quilt Top

1 Tape the *In the Back Country* pattern from the pattern sheet to a table. Center the fusible web, paper side up, over the pattern and trace the design.

2 Cut an 18" × 20" piece of leading fabric. Press it well to remove puckers and wrinkles.

3 Center the traced design on the wrong side of the leading fabric rectangle.

4 Cover the fusible web with your pressing sheet and fuse, following the web manufacturer's instructions. Be sure all edges are fused well.

5 Let the piece cool then use your rotary cutter, scissors or art knife to cut the open areas of the design.

Be sure to cut smooth curves and maintain the ¼" leading lines. Use a ruler when cutting the straight lines of the design.

IN THE BACK COUNTRY · *Designed and made by Susan* · *Finished size: 19¾" × 22½"*

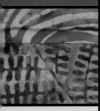

6 From each of the focus fabrics, cut one rectangle:

Very light: 3½" × 14"

Light: 3" × 14"

Medium light: 3" × 14"

Medium: 3" × 14"

Medium dark: 3" × 14"

Dark: 3½" × 14"

7 Arrange the focus fabrics in order from very light at the top to dark at the bottom. Sew the rectangles together in order with ¼" seam allowances and press the allowances open so the quilt will lie flat.

8 Carefully remove the paper backing and position the leading over the focus fabric on your ironing surface.

Make sure all fusible areas of the leading are positioned over the focus fabric. Also check that all straight lines are straight and that the curves are placed correctly.

9 Cover the piece with your pressing sheet and fuse the leading to the focus fabric. Be careful that you don't move the leading during this step. Let the fused fabrics cool.

10 With the fused fabrics right side up, measure 1½" from the outside edges of the focus fabric (on the tree side, measure 1½" from the outermost branches) and trim the excess leading.

Arrange and sew the rectangles together to make the focus fabric.

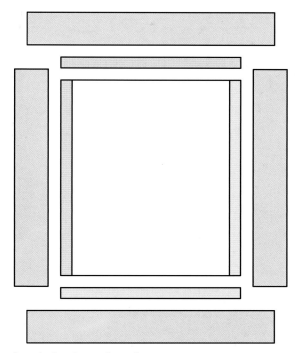

Sew the borders to the quilt.

Adding Borders

1 Cut all strips selvage to selvage. Measure the quilt length. Cut a 1"-wide strip to that measurement from each of two focus fabric remnants. Sew them to the sides of the quilt with ¼" seam allowances. Press the allowances to the outside.

2 Measure the quilt width. Cut a 1"-wide strip to that measurement from each of the same two focus fabric remnants. Sew these strips to the top and bottom. Press the allowances to the outside.

3 For the outer border, cut four strips of leading fabric 2½" wide. Sew these strips to the quilt in the same manner as the inner border. Press the seam allowances toward the inner border.

Quilting and Finishing

1 Cut a piece of leading fabric 23"× 26" for the backing.

2 Sandwich the quilt top, batting and backing together and baste well with safety pins.

3 Thread your sewing machine, in the top and bobbin, with embroidery thread to match the leading fabric. Set your machine to a narrow zigzag stitch.

4 Begin in the center of the quilt and stitch on both edges of each leading line. Remove pins as necessary while you sew.

5 Use a straight stitch and the same embroidery thread to stitch in the ditch on both sides of the inner border.

You may choose to add more detailed quilting on the focus fabric, depending on the designs you want to emphasize.

6 Remove all remaining pins and square up the wall hanging.

7 Cut three strips of leading fabric 2¼" wide for binding. Join the strips on the short ends with 45-degree seams. Press the seam allowances open to reduce bulk.

8 Fold the binding in half lengthwise, wrong sides together, and apply the binding all around the edges of the quilt, mitering the corners.

9 Turn the binding to the back and slipstitch in place by hand.

10 Add a sleeve and label to the back of your wall hanging.

Chapter Five

PANSY BOUQUET PROJECTS

This design is perfect for many floral prints. You can work with just one or pull out all the floral fabrics in your stash and see what you can create for a stunning background. Check your local quilt shop to find what's new!

There are several options for this design. You can use one flower for a little project that will work up quickly or arrange the pansies into a beautiful wreath or spiral design. If you want to see the different effects of moving or rotating the pansy design, take a digital picture and play with it on your computer.

SINGLE PANSY QUILT · *Designed and made by Susan* · *Finished size: 13½" × 13½"*

SINGLE PANSY QUILT

You can view the finished quilt for this project on page 51.

materials

LEADING FABRIC:
1 yd. black cotton, includes outer border, backing and binding

FOCUS FABRIC:
10" × 10"

FUSIBLE WEB:
12" × 12"

LOW−LOFT BATTING:
18" × 18"

MACHINE EMBROIDERY THREAD:
black 60 weight

Making the Quilt Top

1 Tape the *Pansy Wreath* pattern from the pattern sheet to your table with the edge marked "TOP" at the top. Center the fusible web, paper side up, over the pattern and trace the design.

Smoothly trace the curves and use a ruler to trace the straight lines.

2 Cut a 14" square of leading fabric and press it well to remove puckers and wrinkles.

3 Center the traced design on the wrong side of the leading fabric. Cover the fusible web with your pressing sheet and fuse, following the web manufacturer's instructions. Be sure all edges are fused well.

4 Let the piece cool then use your rotary cutter, scissors or art knife to cut the open areas of the design.

Be sure to cut smooth curves and maintain the ¼" leading lines. Use a ruler when cutting the straight lines of the design.

5 Lay the focus fabric, right side up, on your pressing surface and press it well.

6 Carefully remove the paper backing and position the leading over the focus fabric. Move the leading around until you are pleased with the placement.

Make sure all fusible areas of the leading are positioned over the focus fabric. Also check that all straight lines of the design are straight.

7 Cover the piece with your pressing sheet and fuse the leading to the focus fabric. Be careful that you don't move the leading during this step. Let the fused fabrics cool.

8 With the fused fabrics right side up, measure 2½" from the outside edges of the focus fabric and trim the excess fabric.

9 On the wrong side, use sharp scissors to trim away any excess focus fabric that is not fused around the outer edges.

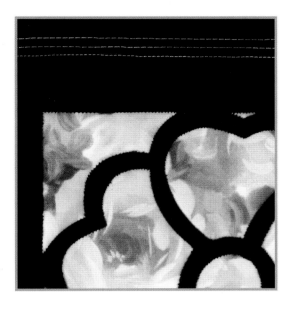

Quilting and Finishing

1 Cut a piece of leading fabric 18" × 18" for the backing.

2 Sandwich the quilt top, batting and backing together and baste well with safety pins.

3 Thread your sewing machine, in the top and bobbin, with embroidery thread to match the leading fabric. Set your machine to a narrow zigzag stitch.

4 Begin in the center of the quilt and stitch on both edges of each leading line. Remove pins as necessary while you sew.

5 Measure 1" from the outside edges of the focus fabric and quilt three lines of stitching around the quilt for a border effect. Use a decorative or variegated thread that matches the focus fabric.

6 Remove all remaining pins and square up the wall hanging.

7 Cut two strips of leading fabric 2¼" wide for binding. Join the strips on the short ends with 45-degree seams. Press the seam allowances open to reduce bulk.

8 Fold the binding in half lengthwise, wrong sides together, and apply the binding all around the raw edges, mitering the corners.

9 Turn the binding to the back and slipstitch it in place by hand.

10 Add a sleeve and label to the back of your wall hanging.

For this project, choose sixteen different floral fabrics in a variety of colors, backgrounds and print styles. If you prefer to use a single focus fabric, see *Pretty in Purple* on page 59.

materials

LEADING FABRIC:
2 yd. green cotton, includes outer border, backing and binding

FOCUS FABRIC:
16 fabrics totaling ⅝ yd.

ACCENT FABRIC FOR INNER BORDER:
⅛ yd.

FUSIBLE WEB:
21" × 21"

LOW-LOFT BATTING:
27" × 27"

MACHINE EMBROIDERY THREAD:
60 weight to match fabric

Floral Wreath · *Designed and made by Susan* · *Finished size: 24¼" × 24¼"*

Making the Quilt Top

1 Tape the *Pansy Wreath* leading pattern from the pattern sheet to your table, with the edge marked "TOP" at the top.

2 Mark two lines, ¼" apart, down the center of the fusible web square. Turn the web and mark another two lines ¼" apart and perpendicular to the first lines.

3 Trace the pansy pattern four times, rotating the fusible web over the leading pattern. Line up the edges with each turn to keep the design even on all four sides. Trim the fusible web 1" from the outer drawn lines.

You could choose either layout option for the placement of the pansy design.

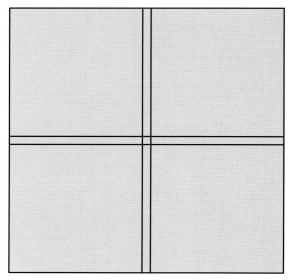

Mark the placement lines for tracing.

The pansy flower can be rotated for different designs.

4 Cut a 22" × 22" piece of leading fabric. Press it well to remove puckers and wrinkles.

5 Center the traced design on the leading fabric. Cover the fusible web with your pressing sheet and fuse, following the web manufacturer's instructions. Be sure all edges are fused well.

6 Let the piece cool then use your rotary cutter, scissors or art knife to cut the open areas of the design.

Be sure to cut smooth curves and maintain the ¼" leading lines, and use a ruler when cutting the straight lines. Make certain the fabrics are correctly oriented.

7 From the variety of focal fabrics, cut the following shapes:

4 squares: 4½" × 4½"

8 rectangles: 4½" × 5½"

4 squares: 5½" × 5½"

If your fabric is directional, make certain all the flowers are going in the same direction before cutting.

8 Arrange the squares and rectangles as shown. Sew them together in rows then sew the rows together with ¼" seam allowances. Press all the allowances open so the quilt will lie flat.

9 Carefully remove the paper backing and position the leading over the focus fabric on your ironing surface. Place the center vertical and horizontal leading lines on top of the center seams of the pieced fabric.

10 Cover the leading with your pressing sheet and fuse the leading to the focus fabric. Be careful that you don't move the leading during this step. Let the fused fabrics cool.

11 With the quilt right side up, measure 1½" away from the outer edges of the focus fabric and trim the excess leading fabric.

5½" SQUARES			
	4 ½" SQUARES		
4 ½" × 5½" RECTANGLES			

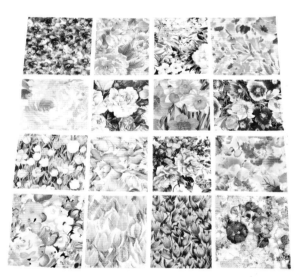

Lay out the cut fabrics in this arrangement.

Adding Borders

1 Cut all strips selvage to selvage. From the accent fabric, cut two strips 1½" wide for the inner border. Measure the quilt length and cut two pieces to that measurement. Sew them to the sides of the quilt. Press the allowances toward the accent strips.

2 Measure the quilt width and cut two pieces to that measurement. Sew them to the top and bottom. Press the allowances toward the accent strips.

3 For the outer border, cut two strips of leading fabric 2¼" wide. Add them to the quilt in the same manner as the accent strips. Press the seam allowances toward the accent strips.

Quilting and Finishing

1 Cut a piece of leading fabric 26" × 26" for the backing.

2 Sandwich the quilt top, batting and backing together and baste well with safety pins.

3 Thread your sewing machine, in the top and bobbin, with embroidery thread to match the leading fabric. Set your machine to a narrow zigzag stitch.

4 Begin in the center of the quilt and stitch on both edges of each leading line. Remove pins as necessary while you sew.

5 Use a straight stitch and the same embroidery thread to stitch in the ditch on both sides of the inner border.

6 Remove all remaining pins and square up the wall hanging.

7 Cut three strips of leading fabric 2¼" wide for binding. Join the strips on the short ends with 45-degree seams. Press the seam allowances open to reduce bulk.

8 Fold the binding in half lengthwise, wrong sides together, and apply the binding all around the raw edges, mitering the corners.

9 Turn the binding to the back and slipstitch it in place by hand.

10 Add a sleeve and label to the back of your wall hanging.

PRETTY IN PURPLE

To make this version, replace the sixteen focus fabrics with one 20" square and follow the instructions for making *Floral* *Wreath* (page 54). Just like the *Wreath* project, these blocks can be rotated to make different designs.

PRETTY IN PURPLE · *Designed and made by Susan* · *Finished size: 24¼" × 24¼"*

Chapter Six

SPINNING WHEEL PROJECTS

Daphne has developed a method for eliminating the need to join pieces of fusible web when creating large designs! She traces the design on smaller pieces of fusible web then arranges and fuses them on one large piece of leading fabric. The following *Spinning Wheel* quilts use Daphne's inventive method and will save you time. Have fun!

SPINNING WHEEL 1 · *Designed and made by Daphne* · *Finished size: 28¾" × 28¾"*

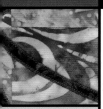

SPINNING WHEEL 1

The design for this wall quilt (shown on page 61) was developed by creating a square leading design then duplicating and rotating the square four times. For this project, choose two focus fabrics, which will be pieced checkerboard fashion. If you prefer to use a single focus fabric, see *Spinning Wheel 2*, on page 66.

materials

LEADING FABRIC
2½ yd. cotton that contrasts with the focus fabrics, includes backing and binding

FOCUS FABRICS:
2 fabrics, ½ yd. each

FUSIBLE WEB:
4 squares, 12" × 12"

LOW-LOFT BATTING:
32" × 32"

MACHINE EMBROIDERY THREAD:
60 weight to match leading fabric

Preparing the Leading

1 Tape the *Spinning Wheel* pattern from the pattern sheet to a table. Be sure the edge marked "TOP" is at the top.

2 Trace the pattern onto the paper side of a fusible web square, leaving ½" on the right and bottom edges and 1½" at the top and left edges. Repeat for the remaining three squares.

Smoothly trace the curves and use a ruler to trace the straight lines.

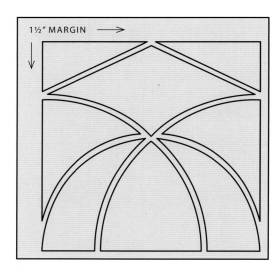

Trace the pattern onto the squares.

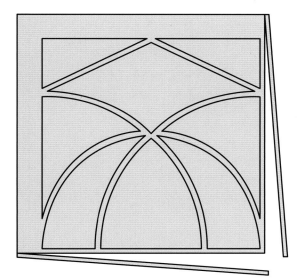

Trim the fusible web, leaving ⅛" outside the traced line on the right and bottom edges.

Draw placement lines to divide your leading fabric into four equal squares.

3 Trim the right and bottom edge of each square to ⅛" from the edge of the design.

4 Cut a 30" square of leading fabric. Press it well to remove puckers and wrinkles.

5 Draw centered vertical and horizontal placement lines on the wrong side of the leading fabric with a white ink marker. These lines will be used to align the traced fusible squares.

Do not press the fabric after drawing the placement lines because the white ink marker will be removed with the heat and steam from your iron.

6 Place one square of fusible web on the wrong side of the leading fabric in the top left area. Line up the trimmed edges of the fusible web with the drawn lines.

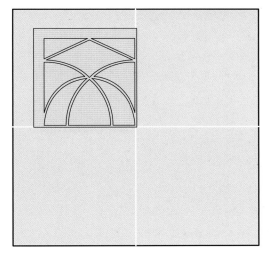

Align the fusible web's edges with the drawn placement lines.

7 Cover the fusible web with your pressing sheet and fuse, following the web manufacturer's instructions. Be sure all edges are fused well.

8 Place a second square of fusible web right next to the first one, turning the square a quarter turn.

The two squares meet will be exactly ¼" apart (⅛" on each square of fusible web).

9 Cover the fusible web with your pressing sheet and fuse. Be sure all edges are fused well.

10 Place and fuse the third and fourth squares of fusible web in the remaining areas, one at a time, turning the squares to continue the established pattern.

11 Let the piece cool. Use your rotary cutter, scissors or art knife to cut the open areas of the design.

Be sure to cut smooth curves and maintain the ¼" leading lines, and use a ruler when cutting the straight lines.

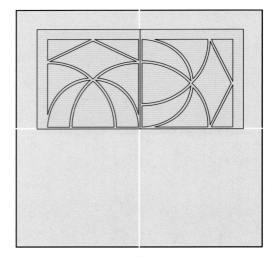

Place the second square of fusible on the leading, rotating it a quarter turn.

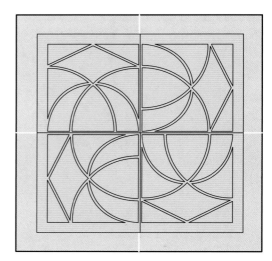

Four squares of fusible web are fused to the square of leading fabric.

Making the Quilt Top

1 Cut the following pieces from each focus fabric:

2 squares: 6½" × 6½"

2 squares: 5½" × 5½"

4 rectangles: 6½" × 5½"

2 Arrange the pieces, as shown, alternating the fabrics. Sew them together with ¼" seam allowances. Press all allowances open.

3 Place the focus fabric piece right side up on your pressing surface. Carefully remove the paper backing and position the leading over the focus fabric. Place the center vertical and horizontal leading lines on top of the center seams of the pieced fabric.

Place a piece of parchment paper on your ironing surface so your quilt will not be fused to the surface (there will be excess fusible around the edges of the focus fabric).

Pieced focus fabric construction.

4 Cover the leading with your pressing sheet and fuse it to the focus fabric. Be careful that you don't move the leading during this step. Let the fused fabrics cool.

5 With the piece right side up, measure 4½" away from the outer edges of the fabric and trim the excess leading fabric.

Quilting and Finishing

1 Cut a 32" × 32" piece of leading fabric for the backing.

2 Sandwich the quilt top, batting and backing together and baste well with safety pins.

3 Thread your sewing machine, in the top and bobbin, with embroidery thread to match the leading fabric. Set your machine to a narrow zigzag stitch.

4 Begin in the center of the quilt and stitch on both edges of each leading line. Remove pins as necessary while you sew.

Daphne used variegated polyester thread (coordinated with the focus fabrics) and a wave stitch to quilt the wide outer border.

5 Remove all remaining pins and square up the wall hanging.

6 Cut four strips of leading fabric 2¼" wide for binding. Join the strips on the short ends with 45-degree seams. Press the seam allowances open to reduce bulk.

7 Fold the binding in half lengthwise, wrong sides together, and apply the binding all around the raw edges, mitering the corners.

8 Turn the binding to the back and slipstitch in place by hand.

9 Add a sleeve and label to the back of your wall hanging.

To make this version of *Spinning Wheel*, replace the two focus fabrics with one 26" square. Again, to avoid the process of joining pieces of fusible web together, trace the design on smaller pieces of fusible web, then arrange and fuse them on one large piece of leading fabric.

materials

LEADING FABRIC:
2½ yd. cotton, includes outer border, backing and binding

FOCUS FABRIC:
⅞ yd.

ACCENT FABRIC FOR INNER BORDER:
¼ yd.

FUSIBLE WEB:
4 squares, 12" × 12"

LOW-LOFT BATTING:
32" × 32"

MACHINE EMBROIDERY THREAD:
60 weight to match leading fabric

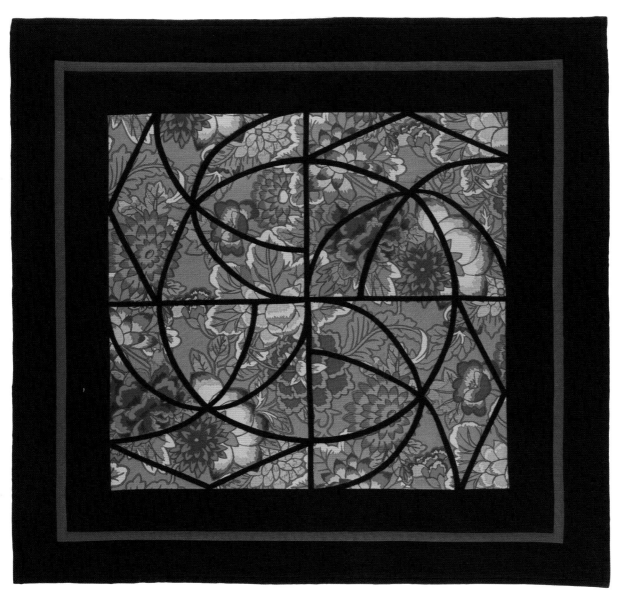

SPINNING WHEEL 2 · *Designed and made by Daphne* · *Finished size: 30¼" × 30¼"*

Preparing the Leading

1 Follow the steps for Preparing the Leading for version 1 on page 62.

Making the Quilt Top

1 Cut a 26" square of focus fabric and press to remove any puckers or wrinkles.

2 Carefully remove the paper backing and position the leading over the focus fabric on your ironing surface. Move the leading around until you are pleased with the placement.

Ensure all straight lines of the design are straight and the curves are placed correctly.

3 Cover the leading with your pressing sheet and fuse the leading to the focus fabric. Be careful that you don't move the leading during this step. Let the fused fabrics cool.

4 With the piece right side up, measure 2½" away from the outer edges of the focus fabric and trim the excess leading and focus fabric.

5 On the wrong side, use sharp scissors to trim away any excess focus fabric that is not fused around the outside edges.

Adding the Borders

1 From the accent fabric, cut four strips 1" wide for the inner border. Measure the quilt length and cut two pieces to that measurement. Sew them to the sides of the quilt. Press the allowances toward the accent strips. Repeat for the top and bottom border strips.

2 For the outer border, cut four 2½" strips of leading fabric. Add them to the quilt in the same manner as the accent strips. Press the seam allowances toward the accent strips.

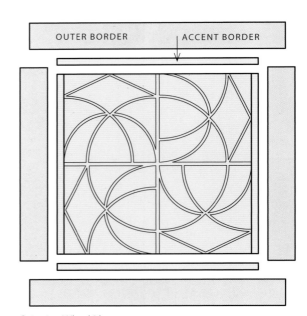

Spinning Wheel 2 layout.

Quilting and Finishing

1 Cut a piece of leading fabric 32" × 32" for the backing.

2 Sandwich the quilt top, batting and backing together and baste well with safety pins.

3 Thread your sewing machine, in the top and bobbin, with the embroidery thread. Set your machine to a narrow zigzag stitch.

4 Begin in the center of the quilt and stitch on both edges of each leading line. Remove pins as necessary while you sew.

5 Stitch in the ditch on both sides of the accent border with a straight stitch and the same embroidery thread. Remove all remaining pins and square up the wall hanging.

6 Cut four strips of leading fabric 2¼" wide for binding. Join the strips on the short ends with 45-degree seams. Press the seam allowances open to reduce bulk.

7 Fold the binding in half lengthwise, wrong sides together, and apply the binding all around the raw edges, mitering the corners.

8 Turn the binding to the back and slipstitch it in place by hand.

9 Add a sleeve and label to the back of your wall hanging.

Chapter Seven

PARIS VIEW PROJECTS

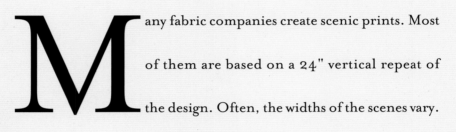

Many fabric companies create scenic prints. Most of them are based on a 24" vertical repeat of the design. Often, the widths of the scenes vary. Other unique fabrics are printed from selvage to selvage, offering a full 40" wide scene. Daphne's design can accommodate all these types of fabric because there are areas where the leading design can be lengthened or shortened. The design is asymmetrical—that is, the top is different from the bottom. This allows more opportunity for design because the top can be flipped and repeated at the bottom and vice versa. The three projects in this chapter explore these options.

SERENITY BRIDGE · *Designed and made by Daphne* · *Finished size: 24" × 30"*

Photographs can be excellent sources of inspiration for your quilting projects. Daphne's design for *Serenity Bridge* is based on a photograph of wrought iron taken in Paris by Lynn Allaire. The finished quilt can be see on page 71.

materials

LEADING FABRIC:
2⅛ yd. black cotton, includes outer border, backing and binding

FOCUS FABRIC:
¾ yd.

ACCENT FABRIC FOR INNER BORDER:
⅛ yd.

FUSIBLE WEB:
18" × 24"

LOW-LOFT BATTING:
28" × 35"

MACHINE EMBROIDERY THREAD:
60 weight, for zigzag stitching
decorative threads to match focus fabric, for quilting

Lynn Allaire's photo of wrought iron, taken in Paris with Daphne's design options.

Making the Quilt Top

1 Tape the *Paris View* pattern from the pattern sheet to your table. Center the fusible web, paper side up, over the pattern and trace the design.

Smoothly trace the curves and use a ruler to trace the straight lines.

2 Cut a 20" × 26" rectangle of leading fabric. Press it well to remove puckers and wrinkles.

3 Center the traced design on the wrong side of the leading fabric. Cover the fusible web with your pressing sheet and fuse following the web manufacturer's instructions. Be sure all edges are fused well.

4 Let the piece cool then use your rotary cutter, scissors or art knife to cut the open areas of the design.

We recommend using a small, sharp pair of scissors for the tight curves and spiral areas of this design. Be sure to cut smooth curves and maintain the ¼" leading lines.

5 Cut a piece of focus fabric 19" × 25". Press to remove any puckers or wrinkles.

6 Carefully remove the paper backing and position the leading over the focus fabric. Move the leading around until you are pleased with the placement. Make sure all the fusible areas of the leading are positioned over the focus fabric. Also ensure all straight lines of the design are straight and that the curves are placed correctly.

7 Cover the piece with your pressing sheet and fuse the leading to the focus fabric. Be careful that you don't move the leading during this step. Let the fused fabrics cool.

8 With the piece right side up, measure 1½" away from the outside edges of the focus fabric on the sides and bottom and trim away any excess fabric. Measure 1½" above the center arch at the top and trim straight across the top.

9 On the wrong side, use sharp scissors to trim away any excess focus fabric that is not fused around the outer edges.

Adding Borders

1 Cut all strips selvage to selvage. From the accent fabric, cut three ¾" strips for the inner border. Measure the quilt length and cut two pieces to that measurement. Sew them to the sides of the quilt. Press the seam allowances toward the accent strips.

2 Measure the quilt width and cut two pieces to that measurement. Sew them to the top and bottom. Press the allowances toward the accent strips.

3 For the outer border, cut four 3" strips of leading fabric. Add them to the quilt in the same manner as the accent strips. Press the allowances toward the accent strips.

Quilting and Finishing

1 Cut a 28" x 35" rectangle of leading fabric for the backing.

2 Sandwich the quilt top, batting and backing together and baste well with safety pins.

3 Thread your sewing machine, in the top and bobbin, with embroidery thread to match the leading fabric. Set your machine to a narrow zigzag stitch.

4 Begin with the innermost leading lines and stitch on both edges of each leading line. Remove pins as necessary while you sew. Pivot frequently when stitching tight areas to make smooth curves.

5 Remove all remaining pins and square up the wall hanging to measure 24" × 30".

6 Quilt the large open areas of the design to hold the quilt layers together. To add emphasis to the accent border, quilt in the ditch on both sides of the border.

Daphne used free-motion machine quilting with matching threads around areas of the focus fabric design. She quilted wavy lines in the trees and followed the shapes of the foliage around the water with green thread. She quilted around the flowers with a variegated orange and fuchsia thread.

7 Cut three strips of leading fabric 2¼" wide for binding. Join the strips on the short ends with 45-degree seams. Press the seam allowances open to reduce bulk.

8 Fold the binding in half lengthwise, wrong sides together, and apply the binding all around the raw edges, mitering the corners.

9 Turn the binding to the back and slipstitch in place by hand.

10 Add a sleeve and label to the back of your wall hanging.

ROSE ARBOR

For her quilt, Daphne chose Rose Arbor fabric by Michael Miller Fabrics and designed the leading to fit the fabric. She repeated the lower half of the leading design at the top and widened the leading to show more of the scene. This project takes you through the steps used to fit the leading design to your fabric scene.

materials

LEADING FABRIC:
1⅝ yd. black cotton, includes Border 4 and binding

FOCUS FABRIC:
⅞ yd.

BORDER 1:
¼ yd.

BORDER 2:
⅛ yd.

BORDER 3:
⅜ yd.

BACKING FABRIC:
1¼ yd.

FUSIBLE WEB:
24" × 24"

LOW-LOFT BATTING:
40" × 40"

MACHINE EMBROIDERY THREAD:
black 60 weight for zigzag stitching
invisible thread for quilting

IMPORTANT NOTE: This Materials list gives requirements for a scene 23" × 23", so you may need more or less fabric, depending on the size of your scene. See Fitting the Pattern, steps 1 and 2, and Making the Quilt Top, step 1, to determine the fabric requirements for your project.

ROSE ARBOR · *Designed and made by Daphne* · *Finished size: 36½" × 36½"*

Fitting the Pattern

1 Measure the design area of your focus fabric. Add 4" to the width and the length and cut the focus fabric.

2 Prepare a piece of fusible web 2" wider and longer than the design area. (Refer to page 12 for joining pieces of fusible web, if needed.)

Daphne's scene measures 22" × 22", so she cut a 26" square of focus fabric and prepared a 24" square of fusible web.

3 Measure 1" in from the edges of the fusible web, with a large square ruler, and use a pencil to draw placement guidelines on the paper side of the web.

Be sure to keep the corners at 90-degree angles when you draw the guidelines to ensure your leading design remains flat.

4 Tape the *Paris View* leading pattern from the pattern sheet to your table. Position the fusible web on top of the leading pattern, lining up the guideline on the fusible web with the lower-left corner of the pattern.

5 Trace the pattern up to the "widen here" and "lengthen here" markings on the pattern.

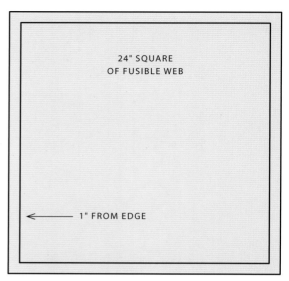

Draw reference lines 1" from the edge of the fusible web.

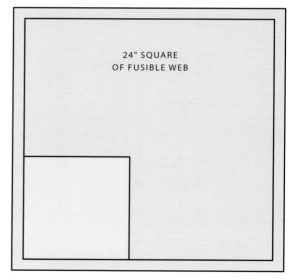

Trace the lower-left corner of the design.

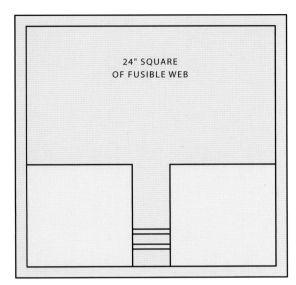

Join the left and right design areas.

6 Move the fusible web to the left and line up the guideline on the fusible web with the lower-right corner of the pattern.

7 Trace the pattern up to the "widen here" and "lengthen here" markings on the pattern. Use a ruler to join the designs at the bottom of the fusible web.

8 Rotate the fusible web so the top of the web is at the bottom. Position the fusible web on top of the leading pattern, again lining up the guideline on the fusible web with the lower left corner of the pattern.

9 Repeat the steps to trace the lower left and the lower right sections of the pattern and to join the design areas. Erase any unnecessary reference lines outside the design. You now have a leading design to fit your focus fabric scene.

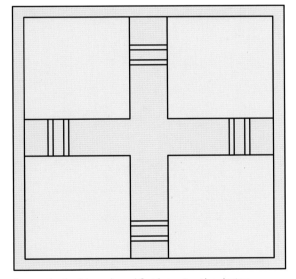

Rotate the fusible web and finish tracing the design.

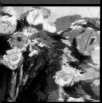

Making the Quilt Top

1 Cut a rectangle of leading fabric 6" wider and longer than the design area. Press it well to remove puckers and wrinkles.

Daphne's design area was 22" × 22", so she cut her leading 28" square.

2 Center the traced design on the wrong side of the leading piece. Cover the fusible web with your pressing sheet and fuse, following the web manufacturer's instructions. Be sure all edges are fused well.

3 Let the piece cool then use your rotary cutter, scissors or art knife to cut the open areas of the design.

We recommend using a small pair of scissors for the tight curves and spiral areas of this design. Be sure to cut smooth curves and maintain the ¼" leading lines.

4 Press the focus fabric piece to remove any puckers or wrinkles.

5 Carefully remove the paper backing and position the leading over the focus fabric on your ironing surface. Move the leading around until you are pleased with the placement.

Make sure all fusible areas of the leading are positioned over the focus fabric. Also ensure all straight lines of the design are straight and the curves are placed correctly.

6 Cover the piece with your pressing sheet and fuse the leading to the focus fabric. Be careful that you don't move the leading during this step. Let the fused fabrics cool.

7 With the piece right side up, measure 2¼" from the outside edges of the focus fabric and trim any excess leading and focus fabric.

8 On the wrong side, use sharp scissors to trim away any excess focus fabric that is not fused around the outer edges.

Adding Borders

1 Cut all strips selvage to selvage.

Daphne added three accent borders to her quilt. For your accent borders, use colors and textures that coordinate with your focus fabric. You can adjust the number and widths of the borders. The middle border is a folded strip, like a flat piping. Here are the measurements Daphne used in her quilt:

Border 1: four 1½" strips

Border 2: four 1" strips

Border 3: four 1¾" strips

Border 4: four 3½" strips

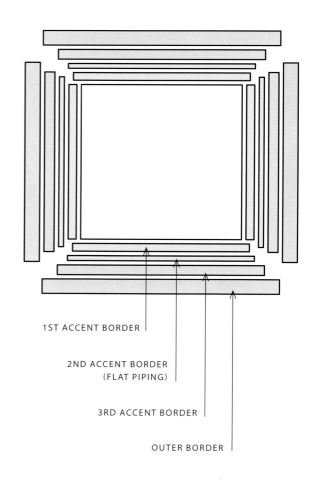

1ST ACCENT BORDER

2ND ACCENT BORDER
(FLAT PIPING)

3RD ACCENT BORDER

OUTER BORDER

Border 1

1 Measure the quilt length. Cut two strips that measurement and sew them to the sides of the quilt. Press the seam allowances toward the border strips.

2 Measure the quilt width, cut two pieces to that measurement and sew them to the top and bottom. Press the seam allowances toward the border strips.

Border 2

1 This border is a flat piping. Fold the 1" strips in half along their length, wrong sides together, and press.

2 Measure the quilt length. Cut two piping strips to that measurement and sew them to the sides of the quilt. Do not press the piping.

3 Measure the quilt width. Cut two piping pieces to that measurement and sew them to the top and bottom. Do not press. The folded piping will lie flat on top of the first border.

Border 3

1 Repeat the measuring, cutting and sewing as for Border 1. Press these seam allowances toward Border 3.

Border 4

1 Repeat the steps for measuring and cutting as before. Press the seam allowances toward Border 4.

Quilting and Finishing

1 Measure your finished quilt top and cut a rectangle of leading fabric 3" wider and longer for the backing. Cut a piece of batting the same size as the backing.

2 Sandwich the quilt top, batting and backing together and baste well with safety pins.

3 Thread your sewing machine, in the top and bobbin, with embroidery thread to match the leading fabric. Set your machine to a narrow zigzag stitch.

4 Beginning with the innermost leading lines, stitch on both edges of each leading line. Remove pins as necessary while you sew.

Pivot frequently when stitching tight areas, to make smooth curves.

5 Remove all remaining pins. Quilt the large open areas of this design to hold the quilt layers together.

Daphne quilted a diamond grid with invisible thread over the center area of the quilt. It's important to quilt evenly over the whole quilt, so she quilted in the ditch of the border seams and quilted a diamond grid in the outer border as well.

6 Cut four strips of leading fabric 2¼" wide for binding. Join the strips together on the short ends with 45-degree seams. Press the seam allowances open to reduce bulk.

7 Fold the binding in half lengthwise, wrong sides together, and apply the binding all around the raw edges, mitering the corners.

8 Turn the binding to the back and slipstitch in place by hand.

9 Add a sleeve and label to the back of your wall hanging.

WEST COAST LANDSCAPE

Daphne chose a landscape fabric by Hoffman California Fabrics for this version of the *Paris View* pattern. This scene is the full width of the fabric, so the design was lengthened to fit the best part of the fabric design. Use the fabric amounts as a guideline and adjust as necessary for your fabric scene.

materials

LEADING FABRIC:
2½ yd. black cotton, includes outer border, backing and binding

FOCUS FABRIC:
⅝ yd. (I yd. if scene extends into borders)

ACCENT FABRIC FOR INNER BORDER:
⅛ yd.

FUSIBLE WEB:
18" × 38"

LOW-LOFT BATTING:
30" × 49"

MACHINE EMBROIDERY THREAD:
60 weight for zigzag stitching

invisible thread for quilting

metallic thread for quilting

75 crystals or beads

IMPORTANT NOTE: This Materials list gives requirements for a scene 16" × 36", so you may need more or less fabric, depending on the size of your scene. See Fitting the Pattern, steps 1 and 2, and Making the Quilt Top, step 1, to determine the fabric requirements for your project.

Fitting the Pattern

1 Measure the design area of your focus fabric. Add 4" to the width and length and cut the focus fabric.

2 Prepare a piece of fusible web 2" wider and longer than the design area. See page 12 for joining pieces of fusible web, if needed.

Daphne's scene measures 16" × 36", so she cut a 20" × 40" rectangle of focus fabric and prepared a piece of fusible web 18" × 38".

3 Measure 1" from the edges of the fusible web, with a large square ruler, and draw placement guidelines with a pencil on the paper side of the fusible web.

Keep the corners at 90 degrees when you draw guidelines to ensure your leading design remains flat.

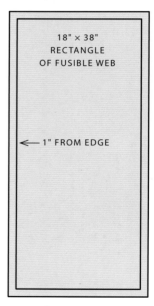

Draw reference lines 1" from the edge of the fusible web.

WEST COAST LANDSCAPE · *Designed and made by Daphne* · *Finished size: 25" × 44¾"*

4 Tape the *Paris View* pattern from the pattern sheet to your table. Position the fusible web on top of the leading pattern, lining up the guideline on the fusible webwith the bottom pattern line.

5 Trace the bottom of the pattern up to the "lengthen here" marking on the pattern sheet.

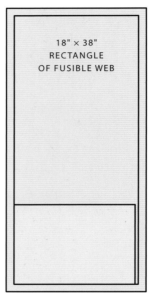

Trace the bottom of the design.

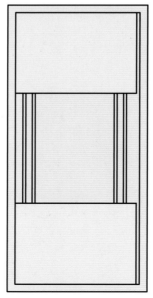

Trace the top of the design and join the design on the sides.

6 Move the fusible down and line up the guideline at the top with the top of the pattern. Trace the top of the pattern to the "lengthen here" marking on the pattern.

7 Use a pencil and ruler to draw the vertical leading lines to join the top and bottom designs. Erase any unnecessary reference lines around the outside of the design. You now have a leading design to fit your focus fabric scene.

Making the Quilt Top

1 Cut a rectangle of leading fabric 2" wider and longer than the fusible web. Press it well to remove puckers and wrinkles.

Daphne's fusible web is 18" × 38", so she cut her leading 20" × 40".

2 Center the traced design on the wrong side of the leading fabric. Cover the fusible web with your pressing sheet and fuse, following the web manufacturer's instructions. Be sure all edges are fused well.

3 Let the piece cool then use your rotary cutter, scissors or art knife to cut the open areas of the design.

We recommend using a small pair of scissors for the tight curves and spiral areas of this design. Be sure to cut smooth curves and maintain the ¼" leading lines.

4 Press the focus fabric piece to remove any puckers or wrinkles.

5 Carefully remove the paper backing and position the leading over the focus fabric on your ironing surface. Move the leading around until you are pleased with the placement.

Make sure all fusible areas of the leading are positioned over the focus fabric. Also ensure all straight lines of the design are straight and the curves are placed correctly.

6 Cover the leading with your pressing sheet and fuse the leading to the focus fabric. Be careful that you don't move the leading during this step. Let the fused fabrics cool.

7 With the piece right side up, measure 1¾" away from the focus fabric on the sides and bottom and trim any excess leading and focus fabric.

8 Measure 1½" above the center arch at the top and trim straight across the top.

Adding Borders

1 Cut all strips selvage to selvage. From the accent fabric, cut three strips 1" for the inner border. Measure the quilt length and cut two pieces to that measurement. Sew them to the sides of the quilt. Press the seam allowances toward the accent strips.

2 Measure the quilt width and cut two pieces to that measurement. Sew them to the top and bottom. Press the allowances toward the accent strips.

3 For the outer border, cut four 3" strips of leading fabric. Sew the strips together, end to end, as necessary to create the needed lengths.

4 Add the outer border to the quilt in the same way as the inner border. Press the seam allowances toward the inner border.

Expanding the Scene

To expand the scene in this design, Daphne selected areas of the same focus fabric to pull out over the borders. She ironed fusible web to the wrong side of the ferns section of another piece of the fabric, cut them out with scissors then fused them in place over the borders.

Quilting and Finishing

1 Measure your finished quilt top and cut a piece of leading fabric 3" wider and longer for the backing. Cut a piece of batting the same size as the backing.

2 Sandwich the quilt top, batting and backing together and baste well with safety pins.

3 Thread your sewing machine, in the top and bobbin, with embroidery thread to match the leading fabric. Set your machine to a narrow zigzag stitch.

4 Begin with the innermost leading lines and stitch on both edges of each leading line. Remove pins as necessary while you sew. Pivot frequently when stitching tight areas to make smooth curves.

5 Quilt the large open area in the design to hold the quilt layers together.

Daphne used free-motion quilting with invisible thread in the center area of the quilt and around the edges of the fused ferns. She quilted in the ditch of the accent border seams. To enhance the West Coast nature of the quilt she quilted rain lines with metallic thread then added a few crystals for raindrops. You could use beads to add this bit of sparkle to your quilt.

6 Cut four strips of leading fabric 2¼" wide for binding. Join the strips on the short ends with 45-degree seams. Press the seam allowances open to reduce bulk.

7 Fold the binding in half lengthwise, wrong sides together, and apply the binding all around the edge, mitering the corners.

8 Turn the binding to the back and slipstitch in place by hand.

9 Add a sleeve and label to the back of your wall hanging.

Chapter Eight

HILLSIDE HOUSES PROJECTS

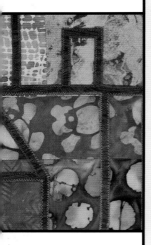

Bright houses perched on a hillside gave us the idea for this quilt. You will see these along the coastlines of Italy and Greece and even in Newfoundland. We've also selected parts of the design to make two smaller quilts. Make the large quilt shown here with a fun array of bright fabrics sewn into one focus fabric or showcase some themed fabrics in one of the smaller versions.

HILLSIDE HOUSES QUILT · *Designed and made by Susan* · *Finished size: 29½" × 36½"*

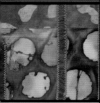

The finished quilt for this project can be seen

on page 85.

materials

LEADING FABRIC:
1⅛ yd., shaded light to dark or a solid color,
includes binding

FOCUS FABRIC:
totaling 1⅝ yd., assorted values light to dark

BACKING FABRIC:
1¼ yd.

FUSIBLE WEB:
24" × 31"

LOW-LOFT BATTING:
34" × 41"

MACHINE EMBROIDERY THREAD:
60 weight to match leading fabric

Making the Quilt Top

1 Tape the *Hillside Houses* pattern from the pattern sheet to your table. Center the fusible web, paper side up, over the pattern and trace the design.

Smoothly trace the curves and use a ruler to trace the straight lines.

2 Cut a 27" × 34" piece of leading fabric. Press it well to remove puckers and wrinkles.

3 Center the traced design on the wrong side of the leading piece. Cover the fusible web with your pressing sheet and fuse, following the web manufacturer's instructions. Be sure all edges are fused well.

4 Let the piece cool then use your rotary cutter, scissors or art knife to cut the open areas of the design.

We recommend using a small sharp pair of scissors for the tight curves of this design. Be sure to cut smooth curves and maintain the ¼" leading lines.

2½" × 6½" RECTANGLE	
3½" × 4½" RECTANGLE	

Make twenty blocks.

5 Arrange your assorted focus fabrics into five piles: light, medium light, medium, medium dark and dark. From each of the five piles, cut four 2½" × 6½" rectangles and eight 3½" × 4½" rectangles. Cut four more dark 2½" × 6½" pieces.

6 Sew two 3½" × 4½" rectangles and one 2½" × 6½" rectangle, as shown, to make one 6½" block. Press all seam allowances open. Make twenty blocks, four of each value from light to dark.

7 Arrange the blocks in five rows with four blocks in each row, with the lightest blocks at the top and the darkest at the bottom. Randomly rotate the blocks to add visual interest. Add the four dark 2½" × 6½" rectangles at the bottom.

8 Sew the blocks and bottom row of rectangles into rows then join all the rows to complete the focus fabric. Press all seam allowances open.

9 Carefully remove the paper backing from the leading and position the leading over the focus fabric on your ironing surface.

10 Cover the leading with your pressing sheet and fuse the leading to the focus fabric. Be careful that you don't move the leading during this step. Let the fused fabrics cool.

11 With the piece right side up, measure 2" from the outside edges of the focus fabric and trim the excess fabrics.

Arrange the blocks and dark rectangles then sew them together.

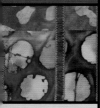

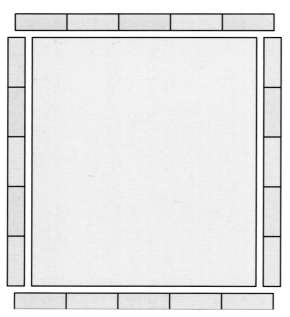

Add borders to the sides, top and bottom of the quilt.

Adding Borders

1 From the focus fabrics, cut the following 2½" × 6½" rectangles: seven light; two each light medium, medium, and medium dark; and nine dark.

2 Join the 2" × 6½" border rectangles at their short ends as follows: five light rectangles for the top border; five dark rectangles for the bottom border; and two strips of six light to dark rectangles for the side borders. Press seam allowances open.

3 Measure the length of the quilt top and cut the two side strips to that measurement. Sew them to the quilt and press the seam allowances toward the border.

4 Measure the quilt width and cut top and bottom strips to that measurement. Sew them to the quilt and press the seam allowances toward the border.

Quilting and Finishing

1 Cut a 34" × 41" rectangle for the backing.

2 Sandwich the quilt top, batting and backing together and baste well with safety pins.

3 Thread your sewing machine with embroidery thread to match the leading fabric. Set your machine to a narrow zigzag stitch.

In the top, Susan used four different shades of gray thread to match the changes in the leading fabric. She used a medium gray thread in the bobbin.

4 Begin in the center of the quilt and stitch on both edges of each leading line. Remove pins as necessary while you sew.

5 Remove all remaining pins and square up the wall hanging.

6 Cut four strips of leading fabric 2¼" wide for binding.

Susan matched the color change in the binding strips to the leading fabric. This may require extra fabric.

7 Fold the four binding strips in half lengthwise, wrong sides together.

8 Measure the length of the quilt and cut two of the binding strips to that measurement. Sew them to the sides of the quilt. Turn the binding to the back and slipstitch it in place by hand.

9 Measure the width of the quilt and cut the two binding strips to that measurement plus ½". Sew them to the quilt, allowing ¼" extra at each end for a turn-under allowance.

10 Turn under the allowance, fold the binding to the back, and slipstitch it in place by hand.

11 Add a sleeve and label to the back of your wall hanging.

IN MY VILLAGE

IN MY VILLAGE · *Designed and made by Susan* · *Finished size: 15¼" × 21¼"*

Susan used a portion of the large *Hillside Houses* design to make this smaller quilt. The section she used is marked with a dashed line on the pattern.

materials

LEADING FABRIC:
1¼ yd. black cotton, includes border, backing and binding

FOCUS FABRIC:
14" × 20"

ACCENT FABRIC FOR INNER BORDER:
⅛ yd.

LOW-LOFT BATTING:
18" × 24"

FUSIBLE WEB:
11" × 17"

MACHINE EMBROIDERY THREAD:
black 60 weight

Making the Quilt Top

1 Tape the *Hillside Houses* pattern from the pattern sheet to your table. Center the fusible web, paper side up, over the *In My Village* section of the pattern and trace the design.

Smoothly trace the curves and use a ruler to trace the straight lines.

2 Cut a 12" × 18" square of leading fabric. Press it well to remove puckers and wrinkles.

3 Center the traced design on the wrong side of the leading fabric.

4 Cover the fusible web with your pressing sheet and fuse, following the web manufacturer's instructions. Be sure all edges are fused well.

5 Let the piece cool then use your rotary cutter, scissors or art knife to cut the open areas of the design.

We recommend using a small sharp pair of scissors for the tight curves of this design. Be sure to cut smooth curves and maintain the ¼" leading lines.

6 Lay the focus fabric, right side up, on your pressing surface and press it well to remove any puckers or wrinkles.

7 Carefully remove the paper backing and position the leading over the focus fabric. Move the leading around until you are pleased with the placement.

Make sure all the fusible areas of the leading are positioned over the focus fabric. Also ensure all straight lines of the design are straight and the curves are placed correctly.

8 Cover the leading with your pressing sheet and fuse the leading to the focus fabric. Be careful that you don't move the leading during this step. Let the fused fabrics cool before moving them.

9 With the piece right side up, measure 1½" away from the outer edges of the focus fabric and trim the excess fabric.

10 On the wrong side, use sharp scissors to trim away any excess focus fabric that is not fused around the outer edges.

Adding Borders

1 Cut all strips selvage to selvage. From the accent fabric, cut two strips 1" wide for the inner border. Measure the length of the quilt top and cut two pieces to that measurement. Sew them to the sides of the quilt. Press the allowances toward the accent strips.

2 Measure the quilt width and cut two pieces to that measurement. Sew them to the top and bottom. Press the seam allowances toward the accent strips.

3 For the outer border, cut two strips of leading fabric 2" wide. Add them to the quilt in the same manner as the accent strips. Press the seam allowances toward the accent border.

Quilting and Finishing

1 Cut an 18" × 24" rectangle of leading fabric for the backing.

2 Sandwich the quilt top, batting and backing together and baste well with safety pins.

3 Thread your sewing machine, in the top and bobbin, with embroidery thread to match the leading fabric. Set your machine to a narrow zigzag stitch.

4 Begin in the center of the quilt and stitch on both edges of each leading line. Remove pins as necessary as you sew the leading lines.

5 Remove all remaining pins and square up the wall hanging.

6 Cut three strips of leading fabric 2¼" wide for binding. Join the strips together on the short ends with 45-degree seams. Press the seam allowances open to reduce bulk.

7 Fold the binding in half lengthwise, wrong sides together, and apply the binding all around the edge, mitering the corners.

8 Turn the binding to the back and slipstitch it in place by hand.

9 Add a sleeve and label to the back of your wall hanging.

Daphne selected a portion of the large *Hillside Houses* design to make a small quilt to showcase a piece of her African fabric collection. The section she used is marked with a dashed line on the pattern.

materials

LEADING FABRIC:
1 yd. black cotton, includes backing and binding

FOCUS FABRIC:
13" × 21"

FUSIBLE WEB:
11" × 19"

LOW-LOFT BATTING:
16" × 24"

MACHINE EMBROIDERY THREAD:
black 60 weight

Making the Quilt Top

1 Tape the *Hillside Houses* pattern from the pattern sheet to a table. Center the fusible web, paper side up, over the *Small Town* section and trace the design.

Smoothly trace the curves and use a ruler to trace the straight lines.

2 Cut a 15" × 24" rectangle of leading fabric. Press it well to remove puckers and wrinkles.

3 Center the traced design on the wrong side of the leading fabric. Cover the fusible with your pressing sheet and fuse, following the web manufacturer's instructions. Be sure all edges are fused well.

4 Let the piece cool then use your rotary cutter, scissors or art knife to cut the open areas of the design.

We recommend using a small sharp pair of scissors for the tight curves of this design. Be sure to cut smooth curves and maintain the ¼" leading lines.

5 Lay the focus fabric, right side up, on your pressing surface and press it well.

6 Carefully remove the paper backing and position the leading over the focus fabric. Move the leading around until you are pleased with the placement.

Make sure all fusible areas of the leading are positioned over the focus fabric. Also check that all straight lines of the design are straight and that the curves are placed correctly.

7 Cover the leading with your pressing sheet and fuse the leading to the focus fabric. Be careful that you don't move the leading during this step. Let the fused fabrics cool.

8 With the piece right side up, measure 2" away from the focus fabric on all sides and trim away any excess leading and focus fabric.

9 On the wrong side, use sharp scissors to trim away any excess focus fabric that is not fused around the outer edges.

Quilting and Finishing

1 From the leading fabric, cut a 16" × 24" piece for backing.

2 Sandwich the quilt top, batting and backing together and baste well with safety pins.

3 Thread your sewing machine, in the top and bobbin, with embroidery thread to match the leading fabric. Set your machine to a narrow zigzag stitch.

4 Begin in the center of the quilt and stitch on both edges of each leading line. Remove pins as necessary while you sew.

5 Remove all remaining pins and square up the wall hanging.

6 Cut two strips of leading fabric 2¼" wide for binding. Join the strips together on the short ends with 45-degree seams. Press the seam allowances open to reduce bulk.

7 Fold the binding in half lengthwise, wrong sides together, and apply the binding all around the edge, mitering the corners.

8 Turn the binding to the back and slipstitch it in place by hand.

9 Add a sleeve and label to the back of your *Small Town*.

SMALL TOWN · *Designed and made by Daphne* · *Finished size: 13" × 21¼"*

Chapter Nine

MOSAIC TILE PROJECTS

Daphne found this design while on a teaching trip. Her hostess's home, on a lake in northern Ontario, had a large fireplace in the living room. The brickwork included decorative metal vents with this grid design. Daphne took a photograph of a vent and set it aside in her design file.

She decided the design was perfect for these projects, which include a 16" pillow, a wall hanging and a tote bag. Fabric options for these pieces are numerous. Choose colors to match your décor for the pillow or wall hanging, and try some fun prints for the tote bag, which you can use to carry your purchases home from the quilt store.

Mosaic Tile · *Designed and made by Daphne* · *Finished size: 39¾" × 51¼"*

Daphne adapted our Too Easy technique to make it easier to create a larger quilt. In this project, some zigzag stitching is done on individual blocks. View the finished quilt for this project on page 95.

materials

LEADING FABRIC:
3⅝ yd. black cotton, includes binding

FOCUS FABRIC:
1⅜ yd. each of two fabrics

BACKING FABRIC:
2⅝ yd.

FUSIBLE WEB:
12 squares, 12" × 12"

LOW-LOFT BATTING:
44" × 55"

MACHINE EMBROIDERY THREAD:
black 60 weight

Making the Blocks

1 Tape the *Mosaic Tile* pattern from the pattern sheet to a table. Trace the pattern onto the paper side of each fusible web square, centering the design.

Smoothly trace the curves and use a ruler to trace the straight lines.

2 From the leading fabric, cut twelve 18" squares. Press them well.

3 For each block, center a fusible web square on the wrong side of a leading square. Cover the fusible with your pressing sheet and fuse, following the manufacturer's instructions. Be sure all edges are fused well.

4 Let the squares cool then use your rotary cutter, scissors or art knife to cut the open areas of the design.

Cut smooth curves and maintain the ¼" leading lines, use a ruler when cutting the straight lines.

5 From each focus fabric, cut six 14" squares; press.

6 For each block, carefully remove the paper backing and position a leading square over a focus fabric square on your ironing surface.

Ensure all the straight lines of the design are straight and the curves are placed correctly.

7 Cover the piece with your pressing sheet and fuse the leading to the focus fabric. Be careful that you don't move the leading during this step. Let the fused fabrics cool.

8 Thread your sewing machine, in the top and bobbin, with embroidery thread. Set your machine to a narrow zigzag stitch.

Zigzag all the leading edges except the outside edges.

9 Zigzag all the leading edges, except the outer straight edges, on each block. These outer edges will be sewn later.

You may need to use a lightweight tear-away stabilizer under each square. It will prevent puckering of the fabric while you zigzag the leading. Gently tear away the stabilizer when you have finished the stitching, before you continue making the quilt top.

Assembling the Quilt

1 Referring to the illustration for measurements and placement, trim and arrange the stained glass blocks.

Using the trim widths shown will result in a ¼" leading between all the squares.

2 Sew the blocks together, matching the stained glass leading at the seam lines. Press all seam allowances open.

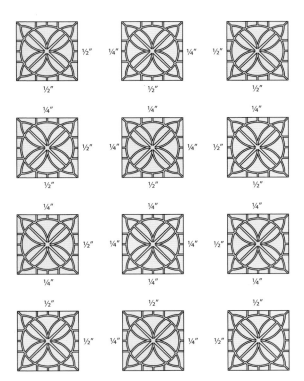

Trim and arrange the stained glass squares.

3 Trim the excess leading around the quilt, 3" away from the outer edges of the focus fabric.

4 On the wrong side, use sharp scissors to trim away any excess focus fabric that is not fused around the outer edges.

Quilting and Finishing

1 Sandwich the quilt top, batting and backing together and baste well with safety pins.

2 Zigzag the outer straight edges of the leading fabric to complete the zigzag stitching. A walking foot is preferred for this step.

3 With a walking foot and black embroidery thread, use a straight stitch to quilt on both sides of all the leading lines.

4 From the leading fabric, cut five 2¼" wide strips, selvage to selvage, for binding.

5 Join the binding strips on the short ends with 45-degree seams. Press the seam allowances open to reduce bulk.

6 Fold the binding in half lengthwise, wrong sides together, and apply the binding all around the edge, mitering the corners.

7 Turn the binding to the back and slipstitch it in place by hand.

8 Add a sleeve and label to the back of your wall hanging.

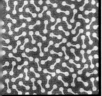

MOSAIC TILE PILLOW

materials

LEADING FABRIC:
⅝ yd. black cotton, includes lining

FOCUS FABRIC:
14" × 14"

BORDER:
⅞ yd., includes pillow back

FUSIBLE WEB:
1 square, 12" × 12"
2 strips, 1½" × 17"

THIN BATTING:
20" × 20"

MACHINE EMBROIDERY THREAD:
black 60 weight
neutral thread for sewing seams

PILLOW FORM:
16" × 16"
3 buttons, 1"

4 Let the piece cool then use your rotary cutter, scissors or art knife to cut the open areas of the design.

Cut smooth curves and maintain the ¼" leading lines. Use a ruler when cutting the straight lines.

5 Press the focus fabric square to remove any puckers or wrinkles.

6 Carefully remove the paper backing and position the leading over the focus fabric, right side up, on your ironing surface, matching the outer edges.

Ensure all straight lines of the leading design are straight and the curves are placed correctly.

7 Cover the leading with your pressing sheet and fuse the leading to the focus fabric. Be careful that you don't move the leading during this step. Let the fused fabrics cool.

8 With the pillow front right side up, measure 1¼" away from the outside edges of the focus fabric and trim the excess fabric. Your piece should measure 13¾" square.

Making the Pillow Front

1 Tape the *Mosaic Tile* leading pattern from the pattern sheet to your table. Center the fusible web square, paper side up, over the pattern and trace the design.

Trace the curves smoothly, and use a ruler to trace the straight lines.

2 Cut a 14" square of leading fabric. Press it well to remove puckers and wrinkles.

3 Center the traced design on the wrong side of the leading square. Cover the fusible web with your pressing sheet and fuse, following the web manufacturer's instructions. Be sure all edges are fused well.

Adding Borders

1 From the border fabric, cut two strips 2¾" wide, selvage to selvage. From these strips cut two 13¾" lengths and two 18¼" lengths for the border.

2 Sew the shorter strips to two opposite sides of the pillow. Press the seam allowances toward the border.

3 Sew the longer border strips to the two remaining sides. Press the allowances toward the border.

MOSAIC TILE PILLOW · *Designed and made by Daphne* · *Finished size: 16" × 16"*

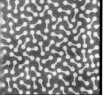

Quilting the Pillow Front

1 Cut a 20" square of leading fabric for the lining.

2 Sandwich the pillow top, batting and lining together and baste well with safety pins.

3 Thread your sewing machine, in the top and bobbin, with the embroidery thread. Set your machine to a narrow zigzag stitch.

4 Begin in the center of the stained glass design and stitch on both edges of each leading line. Remove pins as necessary as you sew the leading lines.

5 Stitch in the ditch of the border seams with a straight stitch and the same embroidery thread. Also stitch ¼" from the edge of the pillow front.

6 Remove all remaining pins and square up the pillow front, cutting off excess batting and lining.

Making the Pillow Back

1 From the leading fabric, cut two rectangles 12" × 18¼" for the pillow back.

2 To add buttons to the pillow back, fold 2" to the wrong side on one long edge of a rectangle and press the fold.

3 Unfold the fabric and position a 1½" × 17" strip of fusible web on the wrong side of the rectangle, placing the strip ¼" from the one long edge and ⅝" from the sides. Cover with your pressing sheet and fuse in place.

This layer of fusible web will stabilize the edges when you stitch the buttonholes and sew on the buttons.

4 Remove the backing paper and turn the ¼" raw edge over the edge of the fusible web and finger press to hold.

Prepare the edge for buttons and buttonholes.

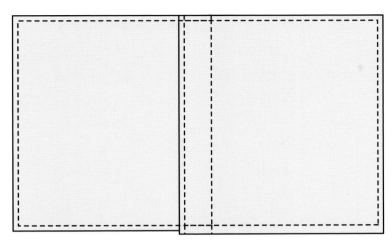

Join the pillow front and pillow back rectangles.

5 Turn down the edge on the pressed fold, so the fusible web is sandwiched between the layers, then fuse. Stitch ¼" from both folded edges.

6 Prepare the second pillow back rectangle in the same way.

7 Fold one of the rectangles in half to find the center of the fused edge. Mark with a pin. Measure 4¼" from this center mark, on each side, and mark with pins.

8 On each mark, sew a buttonhole, sized to fit your buttons, and spaced between the two rows of edge stitching.

Finishing the Pillow

1 Layer the backing rectangle with the buttonholes, right sides together with the pillow front, matching the three raw edges; pin.

2 Place the second backing rectangle on the pillow front, right sides together, matching the remaining raw edges and overlapping the finished edges of the first backing rectangle; pin.

3 Sew around the outer edge of the pillow with a ½" seam allowance. Stitch again ¼" inside the seam allowance.

4 Trim the excess fabric from the corners and turn the pillow cover right side out.

5 Mark the position for the three buttons and sew the buttons on securely. Insert the pillow form and you're done!

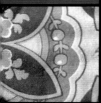

materials

LEADING FABRIC:
1¼ yd. gray cotton, includes lining and handles

FOCUS FABRIC:
½ yd., includes inside pocket

BORDER FABRIC:
⅝ yd., includes tote bag back

THIN MUSLIN:
2 pieces, 20" × 22" (stabilizer for quilting)

FUSIBLE WEB:
12" × 12"

LOW-LOFT BATTING:
2 rectangles, 20" × 22"

2 strips, 1" × 30"

FAST2FUSE:
2 rectangles, 3" × 13½"

MACHINE EMBROIDERY THREAD:
60 weight to match leading

gray piecing thread for seams

invisible polyester thread for machine quilting

Making the Tote Bag Front

1 Tape the *Mosaic Tile* pattern from the pattern sheet to a table. Center the 12" fusible web square, paper side up, over the pattern and trace the design.

Smoothly trace the curves and use a ruler to trace the straight lines.

2 Cut a 14" square of gray leading fabric. Press it well to remove puckers and wrinkles.

3 Center the traced fusible square on the wrong side of the leading fabric. Cover the fusible web with your pressing sheet and fuse, following the web manufacturer's instructions. Be sure all edges are fused well.

4 Let the piece cool then use your rotary cutter, scissors or art knife to cut the open areas of the design.

Be sure to cut smooth curves and maintain the ¼" leading lines. Use a ruler when cutting the straight lines of the design.

5 Cut a 14" square of focus fabric and press to remove any puckers or wrinkles.

6 Carefully remove the paper backing. Position the leading over the focus fabric on your ironing surface.

Be sure to match the outer edges. Also ensure all straight lines of the leading design are straight and the curves are placed correctly.

7 Cover the leading with your pressing sheet and fuse the leading to the focus fabric. Be careful that you don't move the leading during this step. Let the fused fabrics cool.

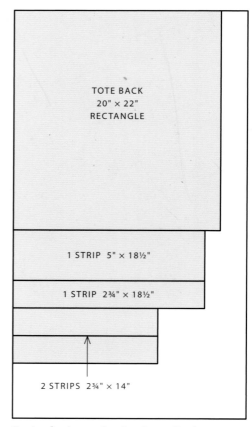

Cutting for the tote bag border and back.

MOSAIC TILE TOTE BAG · *Designed and made by Daphne* · *Finished size: 17" × 17"*

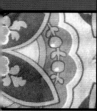

Add borders to the tote bag front.

Adding Borders

1 From the border fabric, cut two 2¾" × 14" strips, one 2¾" × 18½" strip, and one 5" × 18½" strip for the border, and one 20" × 22" rectangle for the tote bag back.

2 Sew the shorter border strips to the sides of the tote bag front. Press the seam allowances toward the border.

3 Sew the 2¾" border to the top and the 5" border to the bottom. Press the seam allowances toward the border.

Topstitch with invisible thread.

Quilting the Tote Bag Front

1 Sandwich the tote bag front, batting and muslin together and baste well with safety pins.

2 Thread your sewing machine, in the top and bobbin, with embroidery thread to match the leading fabric. Set your machine to a narrow zigzag stitch.

3 Begin in the center of the stained glass design and stitch on both edges of each leading line. Remove pins as necessary while you sew.

4 Stitch in the ditch of the border seams with a straight stitch and the same embroidery thread. Stitch again ¼" from the edge of the pillow top.

5 Use invisible thread to topstitch ¾" and 1" from the seam lines inside the border. Mark and stitch a 2" diamond grid below the lower row of topstitching in the wide bottom border. Remove all remaining pins. Do not trim to square up yet.

Making the Tote Bag Back

1 Cut a 20" × 22" rectangle from the border fabric for the tote bag back and mark a 2" diamond grid on the rectangle.

2 Sandwich the tote bag back, batting and muslin together and baste well with safety pins.

3 Thread your sewing machine with invisible thread on the top and neutral thread in the bobbin. Quilt through all three layers on the marked diamond grid.

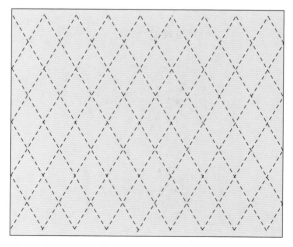

Mark a diamond grid on the tote bag back fabric.

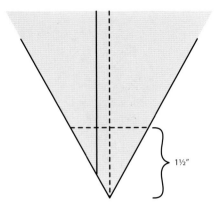

Stitch the bottom corners.

Finishing the Tote Bag Outside

1 Trim the tote bag front and back to 18" wide × 20" long.

2 Layer the pieces, right sides together, and sew around the sides and the bottom with a ½" seam allowance. Sew again close to the first stitching to reinforce the seam.

3 To make a flat bottom for the tote bag, with the bag inside out, align a side seam with the bottom seam. Measure 1½" from the corner and draw a line perpendicular to the seam line.

4 Sew on the marked line. Do not trim to the sewing line. Repeat for the other bottom corner.

Making the Pocket

1 Cut one 8½" × 12" rectangle of focus fabric for the inside pocket.

2 Fold the pocket rectangle in half, right sides together, as shown. Sew around three sides, leaving an opening at the bottom.

3 Trim the bottom corners close to the stitching and turn the pocket right side out.

4 Press it flat and stitch around the pocket, close to the edge and catching the opening in the stitching.

5 Layer the two lining rectangles right sides together and sew around three sides with a 1½" seam, leaving a 9" opening along the bottom.

6 Sew the corners in the lining bottom as you did for the outside bottom.

7 From the leading fabric, cut two 18" × 19½" rectangles for the lining.

8 Pin the pocket to the right side of one lining rectangle, 4" from the top and centered horizontally.

9 Top stitch the pocket in place by sewing over the edge stitching on the sides and bottom. Reinforce the top edge by backstitching.

10 Sew down the center of the pocket through all layers to make two pockets.

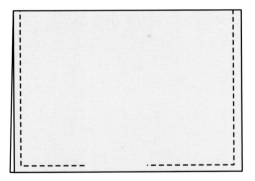

Fold and sew the pocket.

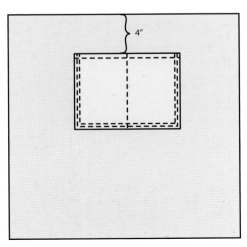

Sew the pocket to the lining.

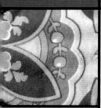

Adding the Handles

1 From the gray cotton, cut two 3" x 32" strips for the handles.

2 Fold in ¼" on the long sides of both handle strips and press. Cut two 1" × 30" strips of thin batting.

3 Working with one handle at a time, open one folded edge and place a 1" × 30" thin batting strip along the fold line and hold it in place with a few pins.

4 Refold the ¼" edge and fold the handle in half, along its length, so both folds meet. Sew close to the edge with gray thread, removing pins as you sew.

5 Sew the opposite edge close to the fold. Sew two more times ¼" away from each line of edge stitching, for a total of four rows of stitching.

Stitch the handles.

6 Repeat the steps to make the second handle. Trim both handles to measure 31" or shorten them to your preferred length.

7 At the top of the tote bag front, measure 4½" from each corner and pin the ends of one handle strip in place, matching the raw edges. Do not twist the handle.

8 Sew ¼" from the raw edge then sew again to reinforce the handles.

9 Measure, place and sew the other handle to the tote bag back in the same way.

Add handles to tote bag front and back.

Tack the bag bottom into the tote bag.

Making the Tote Bottom

1 From the gray leading fabric, cut two pieces 3½" × 14" for the bottom lining.

2 Sandwich two layers of Fast2Fuse between the two pieces of lining, centering the fusible web on the fabric. Press with steam to fuse all three layers.

3 Trim the overhanging lining and zigzag around all edges.

4 Place the bag bottom into the tote bag under the corner triangles at both sides. Tack the corner triangles to the bag bottom, sewing them by hand.

5 Place the lining over the tote bag outside, right sides together, matching the top raw edges and placing the pocket at the back of the tote bag. Keep the handles between the two layers.

6 Sew around the top of the tote bag top with a ½" seam allowance. Stitch again ¼" away from the first seam.

7 Pull the tote bag right side out through the opening at the bottom of the lining.

8 Sew the opening in the lining closed. Push the lining inside the tote bag and press.

9 Pin the top edge. Topstitch around the top edge ¼" from the edge and again ⅜" from the edge.

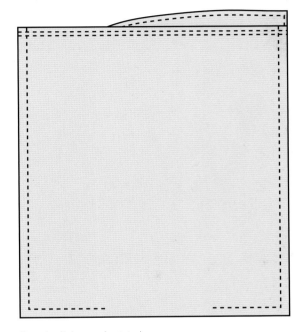
Sew the lining to the tote bag.

Chapter Ten

ROSE WINDOW PROJECTS

Whenever you think "stained glass window," you may think of magnificent windows in churches. You may have pictorial stained glass windows in your place of worship. One of the most spectacular church window styles is the rose window, which is mainly found in churches of the Gothic architectural style—the architecture of many of the great cathedrals in Europe and North America.

The design for this wall quilt was developed with computer software. Daphne modified a whole-cloth dahlia design to create the main leading lines for her *Rose Window* quilt.

ROSE WINDOW WALL HANGING · *Designed and made by Daphne* · *Finished size: 25" × 25"*

View the finished quilt for this project on

page 109.

materials

LEADING FABRIC:
2 yd. black cotton, includes backing and binding

FOCUS FABRIC:
¾ yd.

FUSIBLE WEB:
22" × 22"

LOW-LOFT BATTING:
30" × 30"

MACHINE EMBROIDERY THREAD:
black 60 weight

Making the Quilt Top

1 Tape the *Rose Window* pattern from the pattern sheet to your table. Center the fusible web, paper side up, over the pattern and trace the design.

Smoothly trace the curves and use a ruler to trace the straight lines.

2 Cut a 26" square of leading fabric. Press it well to remove puckers and wrinkles.

3 Center the traced design on the wrong side of the leading fabric. Cover the fusible web with your pressing sheet and fuse, following the web manufacturer's instructions. Be sure all edges are fused well.

4 Let the piece cool then use your rotary cutter, scissors or art knife to cut the open areas of the design.

Be sure to cut smooth curves and use a ruler when cutting the straight lines of the design. Also be sure to maintain the ¼" leading lines.

5 Cut a 24" square of focus fabric. Lay the fabric, right side up, on your pressing surface and press it well to remove any puckers or wrinkles.

6 Carefully remove the paper backing and position the leading over the focus fabric. Move the leading around until you are pleased with the placement.

Make sure all fusible areas of the leading are positioned over the focus fabric. Also check that all straight lines of the design are straight and the curves are placed correctly.

7 Cover the piece with your pressing sheet and fuse the leading to the focus fabric. Be careful that you don't move the leading during this step. Let the fused fabrics cool.

Quilting and Finishing

1 Cut a 30" square of leading fabric for the backing.

2 Sandwich the quilt top, batting and backing together and baste well with safety pins.

3 Thread your sewing machine, in the top and bobbin, with the embroidery thread. Set your machine to a narrow zigzag stitch.

4 Begin in the center of the quilt and stitch on both edges of each leading line. Remove pins as necessary while you sew.

5 Remove all remaining pins and square up the wall hanging to measure 25" × 25".

6 Cut three strips of leading fabric 2¼" wide for binding. Join the strips on the short ends with 45-degree seams. Press the seam allowances open to reduce bulk.

7 Fold the binding in half lengthwise, wrong sides together, and apply the binding all around the edge, mitering the corners.

8 Turn the binding to the back and slipstitch in place by hand.

9 Add a sleeve and label to the back of your wall hanging.

Daphne wanted to make a table runner to coordinate with her *Rose Window* wall hanging. She selected a center section of the design to repeat three times along the length of the runner and centered three focus fabric motifs cut from the same focus fabric used for the wall hanging. She used the same black cotton for both projects.

materials

LEADING FABRIC:
1³⁄₈ yd. black cotton, includes backing
and binding

FOCUS FABRIC:
3 different squares, 11½" × 11 ½" or 1 rectangle,
11½" × 37"

FUSIBLE WEB:
3 squares, 11" × 11"

LOW-LOFT BATTING:
18" × 41"

MACHINE EMBROIDERY THREAD:
black 60 weight

Making the Quilt Top

1 Mark the center of each square of fusible web by drawing vertical and horizontal lines through the center of each square.

2 Tape the *Rose Window* leading pattern from the pattern sheet to your table. Trace the center section of the pattern onto the paper side of each fusible web square, using the dashed alignment lines to center the design.

This center section of the pattern is outlined with a dashed line. Smoothly trace the curves and use a ruler to trace the straight lines.

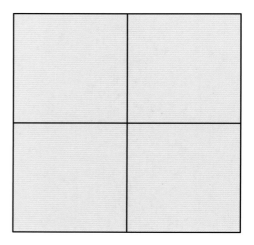

Mark the center lines on the fusible web squares.

Trace the pattern onto the fusible web squares, centering the design.

MINI ROSE TABLE RUNNER · *Designed and made by Daphne* · *Finished size: 15" × 38"*

Mark the center of the leading fabric.

3 Cut a 16" × 40" piece of leading fabric. Press it well to remove puckers and wrinkles.

4 On the wrong side of the leading piece, use a fabric marker to draw vertical and horizontal lines through the center.

5 Place one traced fusible square on the wrong side of the leading fabric, matching the marked center lines.

6 Place the two remaining fusible squares, one on each side of the center square, matching the centering lines. The edges of the fusible squares should touch each other but not overlap.

7 Cover the fusible web squares with your pressing sheet and fuse, following the web manufacturer's instructions. Be sure all edges are fused well.

8 Let the piece cool then use your rotary cutter, scissors or art knife to cut the open areas of the three designs.

Be sure to cut smooth curves. Use a ruler when cutting the straight lines of the design and be sure to maintain the ¼" leading lines.

9 Carefully remove the paper backing. Position the leading over the focus fabric on your ironing surface.

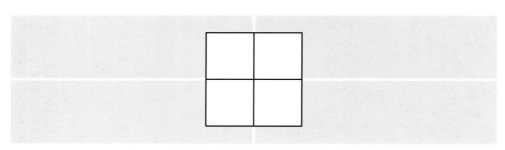

Center a fusible square on the leading fabric.

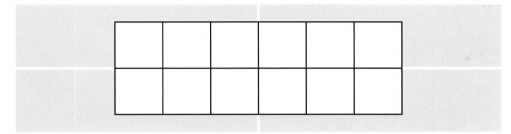

Place the two remaining fusible squares on both sides of the center square.

10 Center the design on the focus fabric squares, if you have selected that option.

Make sure all fusible areas of the leading are positioned over the focus fabric. Ensure all straight lines of the design are straight and that the curves are placed correctly.

11 Cover the leading with your pressing sheet and fuse the leading to the focus fabric. Be careful that you don't move the leading during this step. Let the fused fabrics cool.

12 On the wrong side, use sharp scissors to trim away any excess focus fabric that is not fused around the outer edges.

Quilting and Finishing

1 Cut an 18" × 41" piece of leading fabric for the backing.

2 Sandwich the quilt top, batting and backing together and baste well with safety pins.

3 Thread your sewing machine, in the top and bobbin, with embroidery thread. Set your machine to a narrow zigzag stitch.

4 Begin in the center of the runner and stitch on both edges of each leading line. Remove pins as necessary while you sew.

5 Remove all remaining pins. With the piece right side up, measure 2½" away from the focus fabric on the side edges and trim through all layers. Measure 3" away from the focus fabric on the ends and trim through all layers.

6 Cut three strips of leading fabric 2¼" wide for binding.

7 Join the strips together on the short ends with 45-degree seams. Press the seam allowances open to reduce bulk.

8 Fold the binding in half lengthwise, wrong sides together, and apply the binding all around the edge, mitering the corners.

9 Turn the binding to the back and slipstitch it in place by hand.

PRINCESS ROSE

Daphne was still intrigued by the *Rose Window* design and wanted to use another area of the design for a small project. She also wanted to use a multicolored leading fabric. She decided to "reverse" the fabrics for this project by using black cotton as the focus fabric.

materials

LEADING FABRIC:
¾ yd. cotton, includes backing and binding

FOCUS FABRIC:
15" × 15"

FUSIBLE WEB:
15" × 15"

LOW-LOFT BATTING:
21" × 21"

MACHINE EMBROIDERY THREAD:
60 weight to match leading fabric

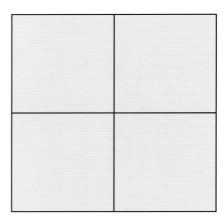

Mark center lines on the fusible web squares.

Trace the pattern onto the fusible web squares.

Making the Quilt Top

1 Mark the center of the square of fusible web by drawing a vertical and a horizontal line through the center.

2 Tape the *Rose Window* leading pattern to your table. Trace the center section, outlined with a double dash, onto the paper side of the fusible web square. Rotate the fusible web until there are two petal shapes on both sides of the square.

For this design, several leading lines in the center of the pattern were removed. The lines to follow when tracing are marked with a double dashed line. Smoothly trace the curves and use a ruler to trace the straight lines.

3 From the leading fabric, cut a 19" square. Press it well to remove puckers and wrinkles.

4 Center the traced design on the wrong side of the leading square. Cover the fusible web with your pressing sheet and fuse, following the web manufacturer's instructions. Be sure all edges are fused well.

5 Let the piece cool then use your rotary cutter, scissors, or art knife to cut the open areas between the leading.

Be sure to cut smooth curves and use a ruler when cutting the straight lines. Also be sure to maintain the ¼" leading lines.

6 Carefully remove the paper backing. Position the leading over the focus fabric on your ironing surface.

PRINCESS ROSE · *Designed and made by Daphne* · *Finished size: 17¾" × 17¾"*

Make sure all fusible areas of the leading are positioned over the focus fabric. Also ensure that all straight lines of the design are straight and the curves are placed correctly.

7 Cover the leading with your pressing sheet and fuse the leading to the focus fabric. Be careful that you don't move the leading during this step. Let the fused fabrics cool.

Quilting and Finishing

1 Cut a 21" square of leading fabric for the backing.

2 Sandwich the quilt top, batting and backing together and baste well with safety pins.

3 Thread your sewing machine, in the top and bobbin, with embroidery thread. Set your machine to a narrow zigzag stitch.

4 Begin in the center of the quilt and stitch on both edges of each leading line. Remove pins as necessary while you sew.

5 Remove all remaining pins and square up the wall hanging to measure 17½" square.

6 Cut two strips of leading fabric 2¼" wide for the binding. Join the strips on the short ends with 45-degree seams. Press the seam allowances open to reduce bulk.

7 Fold the binding in half lengthwise, wrong sides together, and apply the binding all around the edges, mitering the corners.

8 Turn the binding to the back and slipstitch in place by hand.

9 Add a sleeve and label to the back of your wall hanging.

Chapter Eleven

OTHER FUN PROJECTS

The projects in this chapter are guaranteed fun for all quilters. Use our Too Easy Stained Glass method to make a playful and colorful child's quilt, as well as little word banners laced with ribbon. Our method is also perfect for making beautiful frames for photos printed on fabric. The creative possibilities are endless. Enjoy!

PLAYTIME ABC · *Designed and made by Susan* · *Finished size: 32" × 40"*

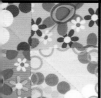

PLAYTIME ABC

This project shows how to use the stained glass method to make a fun child's quilt, along with a bonus banner. Grandma could make them for all of her favorite grandkids! See what other word combinations you can make.

Choose several bright colors for the leading for a different look and have fun with a variety of quilting designs. We've changed the method slightly to make the quilting part easier, so read carefully through all the steps.

You can view the finished quilt on page 119.

materials

LEADING FABRIC:
¾ yd. black cotton, includes binding

FOCUS FABRIC:
assorted small-scale prints, totaling ⅔ yd.
assorted medium-scale prints, totaling 1¼ yd.

BACKING FABRIC:
1½ yd.

FUSIBLE WEB:
20 squares, 4½" × 4½"

LOW-LOFT BATTING:
36" × 44"

MACHINE EMBROIDERY THREAD:
black 60 weight

Trace the letters.

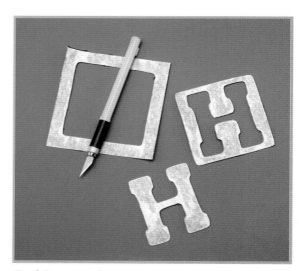

Carefully cut each letter.

Making the Quilt Top

1 Using the following list, trace the number of letters indicated onto the paper side of the fusible web squares. The letters in the pattern are printed in reverse so they will end up facing the right way after fusing.

2 A	1 J	2 P
1 F	2 L	1 R
1 G	1 M	1 S
1 H	2 N	2 U
1 I	1 O	1 Y

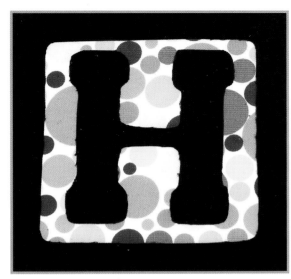
Fuse the leading to each square.

Playtime ABC quilt layout.

2 Cut twenty 4½" squares from the black leading fabric. For each letter, center a traced fusible web square on the wrong side of a square.

3 Cover the fusible web with your pressing sheet and fuse, following the web manufacturer's instructions. Be sure all edges are fused well.

4 Let the pieces cool and use small scissors or an art knife to cut the small leading frames and then the letters. Work carefully to keep all pieces intact without ripping.

5 Cut twenty 4½" squares from the assorted small-scale prints. For each letter, remove the paper backing and center the frame and the letter onto a 4½" small-scale print square.

6 Cover the fusible web with your pressing sheet and fuse the leading to each square, following the web manufacturer's instructions. Be careful that you don't move the leading during this step. Let each piece cool before moving it.

7 Thread your sewing machine, in the top and bobbin, with embroidery thread. Set your machine to a narrow zigzag stitch. Stitch around each frame and letter, sewing carefully around the corners.

8 Following the quilt layout diagram, arrange all the lettered squares to make the words.

9 Cut sixty 4½" squares from the assorted medium-scale prints. Arrange these squares around the lettered squares for a quilt with ten rows of eight squares each.

10 Sew the squares into rows and press the seam allowances open. Then sew the rows together. Press these seam allowances open.

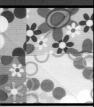

Quilting and Finishing

1 Cut a 36" × 44" piece of fabric for the backing.

2 Sandwich the quilt top, batting and backing together and baste well with safety pins.

3 Quilt through all layers, using an invisible thread on the top and thread to match your backing fabric in the bobbin.

4 Susan quilted a diagonal grid pattern in all the plain squares and stitched around each leading frame and letter.

5 Cut four 2¼" strips of leading fabric for binding. Join the strips on the short ends with 45-degree seams. Press the seam allowances open to reduce bulk.

6 Fold the binding in half lengthwise, wrong sides together, and apply the binding all around the edge, mitering the corners.

7 Turn the binding to the back and slipstitch in place by hand.

8 Add a sleeve and label to the back and enjoy!

Little Banners

Have the family help choose other words such as DOG, HUGS or FUN. Sew the shapes into small quilts and attach them to strips of ribbon with small buttons.

Group other letter combinations to make new words.

PICTURE THIS

Our Too Easy Stained Glass method is perfect for photos printed on fabric. The leading makes a beautiful frame and you can "picture" anything: family, scenery, pets, vacations ... so many choices, so much fun! Choose a coordinating print for the accent border or use a wood-grain fabric for an old-fashioned frame.

Add this beautiful frame to your own picture!

PICTURE THIS · *Designed and made by Susan* · *Finished size: 17" × 19"*

materials

LEADING FABRIC:
1 yd. black cotton, includes backing and binding

**ACCENT FABRIC
FOR BEHIND LEADING:**
¼ yd.

PHOTO TO PRINT ON FABRIC:
8" × 10"

PRINTABLE FABRIC SHEET:
8½" × 11"

FUSIBLE WEB:
15" × 17"

LOW−LOFT BATTING:
18" × 20"

MACHINE EMBROIDERY THREAD:
black 60 weight

Making the Frame

1 Tape the *Picture This* leading pattern from the pattern sheet to your table. Center the fusible web, paper side up, over the pattern and trace the design.

Smoothly trace the curves and use a ruler to trace the straight lines.

2 Cut a 19" × 21" piece of leading fabric. Press it well to remove puckers and wrinkles.

3 Center the traced design on the wrong side of the leading fabric. Cover the fusible web with your pressing sheet and fuse, following the web manufacturer's instructions. Be sure all edges are fused well.

4 Let the piece cool then use your rotary cutter, scissors or art knife to cut the open areas of the design.

Use a ruler when cutting the straight lines of the design and be sure to cut smooth curves and maintain the ¼" leading lines.

5 Follow the manufacturer's directions for preparing and printing your photograph onto the printable fabric sheet. We recommend that you test the printing of your photograph on paper first and make any adjustments before printing the fabric sheet.

Your printed photograph must measure at least 8" × 10" so the accent fabric seams will be under the leading border.

6 Trim your printed fabric to measure exactly 8¼" × 10¼", including the ¼" seam allowances.

7 Cut two 3½" strips of accent fabric. Cut two pieces 10¼" long and sew them to the sides of the photo sheet with ¼" seam allowances.

Trim the print to measure 8¼" × 10¼".

Add accent fabric to the sides and then the top and bottom of the photo.

8 Cut two pieces 14¼" long and sew them to the top and bottom. Press all seam allowances open so they will lie flat under the leading.

9 Carefully remove the paper backing and position the leading over the accent fabric.

Make sure all fusible areas of the leading are positioned over the accent fabric and the straight lines are placed over the seams. Also ensure all straight lines of the design are straight and the curves are placed correctly.

10 Cover the leading with your pressing sheet and fuse the leading to the accent fabric. Be careful that you don't move the leading during this step. Let the fused fabric cool.

11 With the piece right side up, measure 2" away from the accent fabric and trim the excess leading fabric.

Quilting and Finishing

1 Cut a piece of leading fabric 18" × 20" for the backing.

2 Sandwich the quilt top, batting and backing together and baste well with safety pins.

3 Thread your sewing machine, in the top and bobbin, with embroidery thread. Set your machine to a narrow zigzag stitch.

4 Begin on one side of the quilt and stitch on both edges of each leading line. Remove pins as necessary while you sew.

Susan added extra lines of quilting on the black borders for emphasis. You may choose to add more detailed quilting on the picture depending on the designs you wish to emphasize.

5 Remove all remaining pins and square up the wall hanging.

6 Cut three strips of leading fabric 2¼" wide for the binding. Join the strips on the short ends with 45-degree seams. Press the seam allowances open to reduce bulk.

7 Fold the binding in half lengthwise, wrong sides together, and apply the binding all around the edge, mitering the corners.

8 Turn the binding to the back and slipstitch in place by hand.

9 Add a sleeve and label to the back of your wall hanging.

INDEX

FABRICS

Hoffman California Fabrics
Web: www.hoffmanfabrics.com

Michael Miller Fabrics, LLC
Web: www.michaelmillerfabrics.com

Northcott Silk Inc.
Web: www.northcott.net

Red Rooster Fabrics
Web: www.redroosterfabrics.com

TOOLS & SUPPLIES

CM Designs, Inc.
Web: www.addaquarter.com
Add-a-Quarter™ ruler

The Electric Quilt Company
Phone: 800-356-4219
Web: www.electricquilt.com
Quilt design software

Hobbs Bonded Fibers
Phone: 800-433-3357
Web: www.hobbsbondedfibers.com
Batting

Kandi Corp
Phone: 800-985-2634
Web: www.kandicorp.com
Hot Fix Crystals

OLFA - North America Division
Phone: 800-962-6532
Web: www.olfa.com

CUTTING TOOLS

Sanford Corporation
Phone: 800-323-0749
Web: www.sharpie.com
Sharpie® fine point marker

The Warm Company
Web: www.warmcompany.com
Steam-A-Seam 2®

Raggedy Reverse Appliqué

15+ Fast, Fun and Forgiving Quilt Projects

by Kim Deneault

Discover a stress-free new appliqué technique in the detailed instructions and 175 color photos and illustrations of this book. Plus, you'll find 12+ designs for small, quick projects, as well as more complex projects, featured on a pattern insert.

Paperback; 128 pages; 25 b&w illus.; 175 color photos; 0-89689-494-0; 978-0-89689-494-5; Item# Z0765

Appli-Curves

Traditional Quilts with Easy No-Sew Curves

by Elaine Waldschmitt

Create perfect curves every time with this simple technique. Once you've mastered the technique, you can create any of the 12 featured projects. Bonus CD with 20 appliqué templates included.

Paperback; 128 pages; 200 color photos; 0-89689-601-3; 978-0-89689-601-7; Item# Z1659

Rainy Day Appliqué

Quick & Easy Fusible Quilts

by Ursula Michael

Whatever your sewing skill level, you'll enjoy the time and money-saving tips you find in this project-packed guide. Check out the bonus CD with 100+ innovative patterns.

Paperback; 128 pages; 50 b&w photos; 200 color photos; 0-89689-539-4; 978-0-89689-539-3; Item# Z0936

Stitch, Spritz & Sew

Curved Piecing as Easy as 1-2-3

by Kathy Bowers

Easily create unique mirror-image frames and curved pieces without the fuss using water-soluble thread. Includes more than a dozen projects, from bed quilts and lap quilts to wall hangings and crib quilts.

Paperback; 128 pages; 60 color photos; 0-89689-578-5; 978-0-89689-578-2; Item# Z1311

Fun and Fabulous Patchwork & Appliqué Gifts

40 Quick-to-Stitch Projects

by Gail Lawther

With these forty small but perfect projects, quilters will find the inspiration they need to make gifts in an evening or weekend—perfect for presenting to loved ones.

Paperback; 128 pages; 100 color illus. & 50 b&w illus.; 0-7153-2481-0; 978-0-7153-2481-3; Item# Z0873

Discover imagination, innovation and inspiration at www.mycraftivity.com. *Connect. Create. Explore.*